THE ULTIMATE KEY TO HAPPINESS

THE ULTIMATE KEY TO HAPPINESS

HOW TO BE HAPPY ALL THE TIME, NO MATTER WHAT'S GOING ON AROUND YOU

ROBERT SCHEINFELD

ABUNDANCE
PUBLISHING

ISBN: 978-0-9838183-2-8

Printed in the United States of America

10 9 8 7 6 5 4 3 2 1

Books By Robert Scheinfeld

PHASE 1 BOOKS
The Invisible Path To Success
The 11th Element

PHASE 2 BOOKS
Busting Loose From The Money Game
Busting Loose From The Business Game

PHASE 3 BOOKS
The Ultimate Key To Happiness

If you don't know what's meant by Phase 1, Phase 2, and Phase 3, visit this page on the author's website: http://www.robertscheinfeld.com/teachings/

Table Of Contents

Introduction

So …

You want to be happy.

Truly Happy.

All the time.

No matter what's going on around you.

Cool.

That's what I always wanted too.

Discovering how to "get there" was an obsession for me until I finally had the breakthrough I'm sharing with you here.

There are several Big Problems that must be solved before *you* can get there too.

We'll be discussing the Big Problems in detail in the chapters that follow, including how to solve them, but here's a quick summary to get the ball rolling:

1. **What is happiness?** Everyone wants to be happy, or happ*ier*, but few people can precisely define what happiness *really* is. How can you hit a target if you don't know what or where it is?

2. **How important is happiness?** Everyone knows they want to be happy, but few people realize just how important happiness is to them, and how their quest for happiness shapes *everything* they do on a daily basis.

3. **How do I get "there"?** Even if you have an idea what happiness really is, there are few accessible paths that actually lead from where you are now into the True Happiness Experience (despite tons of hype and false claims).

4. **How do I avoid traps and quicksand pits along the way?** Even if you know what True Happiness really is (rare as that is), and even if you're shown a path that can actually take you there (rare as that is), the path has traps and quicksand pits that can prevent you from reaching your desired destination. You must know what these obstacles are, how to avoid them and how to get "unstuck" if you succumb.

5. **Why don't the typical techniques work?** There are zillions of books, audios, videos, courses, events, and workshops offering techniques, strategies, and prescriptions for how to be happy. If we're brutally honest with ourselves, we see that virtually all of them end up being dead ends. You'll continue failing to produce the desired result and driving down dead end after dead end ... until ... you discover *why* the techniques fail and *how* to "turn around" and take a new "road" that really can take you where you want to go.

6. **Why don't the typical therapies work?** The world is filled with therapies, therapeutic models, healing models, and therapists who claim to have the ability to help you be happy or happ*ier*. Once again, if we're brutally honest, we see that virtually all of them fail to deliver the desired result of True Happiness. Until you know *why* they fail, a door will never open to change things.

KEY POINT:

I'm not being critical or judgmental of the products, services, authors, speakers, experts, or therapists I just referred to. I'm simply speaking The Truth about what you see if you look closely at what happens when most people follow those paths.

You should know that prior to making the discoveries shared in this book, I was one of the world's foremost experts on being un-happy.

And one of the world's foremost experts on being angry.

And frustrated.

And depressed.

And feeling hurt.

And feeling like a victim.

I tried everything from the most popular to the most esoteric "woo-woo" solutions in my attempt to feel better.

I took a few baby steps from time to time, which meant there were blips of time when I could say I felt "better," or when something that was making me uncomfortable changed... slightly ... or transformed ... slightly ... or disappeared ... temporarily.

But ultimately, happiness remained elusive.

When I was 46, I had an extraordinary breakthrough. That breakthrough enabled me to see The Truth of things with expanding clarity. I began to see what happiness really was, what it really wasn't, why it remained so elusive (despite all the things I did and tried), and how to consistently enjoy what I now call "True Happiness."

An extraordinary 34-year journey led to that breakthrough.

The story of that journey and breakthrough is shared in my last two books, the New York Times bestseller, *Busting Loose From The Money Game* and *Busting Loose From The Business Game*.

Don't let the titles of those books fool you if you're unfamiliar with them.

While they *are* about money and business from one point of view, they're REALLY about Truth, Consciousness, Spirituality, and solving Life's Greatest Mysteries from a more expanded perspective. Money and business were simply gateways I used to invite people into a discussion of a radically different perspective.

If you're a "Seeker Of Truth," you will find the two *Busting Loose* books to be fascinating, eye-opening, and supportive. However, this book stands on its own. Nothing in my previous books is required to receive maximum benefit from this book.

Beyond what I just shared, I'm not going to chat much about my biography, my credentials, or why you might want to pay close attention to what I share here.

Truth be told, who I am and what I've done doesn't mean much as it relates to being **Truly Happy**.

KEY POINT:

The only thing that matters is what you actually EXPERIENCE during and after reading this book.

I'm going to show you how to prove the Truthfulness of everything I share here – everything – no matter how crazy, far out, counterintuitive, unfamiliar, strange, or wrong it may *seem* to you initially.

Your proof of the Truthfulness and the accuracy of what I'm sharing will come from you looking at, examining, and clearly Seeing what's happening in your own personal experience.

If you're like I was, and like the vast majority of people I've shared these insights with, you'll be shocked by what you see when you look closely at your own experience as it relates to emotions in general, and happiness in specific.

If you're like I was, and like the vast majority of people I've shared these insights with, you'll be shocked by the fact that what I point out has been "hiding in plain sight" all along.

Next, this book is **NOT** about ideas, concepts, theories, or philosophy.

Because everything I share here is based on what you can See in your own personal experience, it's vital that you actually look at what I ask you to look at, see what I'm pointing to, and Ultimately See it.

What do I mean by "See it"?

I mean Seeing from the perspective of Truth, which goes way beyond simply seeing with the eyes or understanding something.

More on this later.

If you simply read the words in this book, look at the content at the theoretical, idea, and concept level only, and you accept ... *or* ... reject it there, you'll miss out on the opportunity of a lifetime.

From one perspective, this book is written in a linear,

sequential way. Each chapter builds on the next. Each chapter provides specific puzzle pieces in a specific order and invites you to assemble them into a specific Big Picture.

I can't control what you do, but in the strongest of voices I can put to paper, I urge you to read this book start to finish, in sequential order, slowly and carefully, and not skip around, skim, or speed read it.

True Happiness is too important to be sacrificed to impatience, being "busy," or old habitual patterns for reading books.

From another perspective, this book is written in a non-linear way.

By that, I mean the opportunity here is to exchange lies, illusions, and stories for Truth.

The lies, illusions, and stories are "hypnotic" in nature and are very convincing. They also have a lot of force or "inertia" behind them. I must support you in being de-hypnotized and overcoming the inertial forces, like a rocket must overcome gravity to soar into space.

I must support you in Seeing what True Happiness really is.

I must support you in taking a quantum leap from where you are now to a new "place."

To provide that kind of support, I've got to blow your mind (literally), fry your circuits, and dynamite lies, illusions, and stories you've thought to be True most or all of your life.

Therefore, as you read the pages that follow, especially the first five chapters, you may feel like you've entered The Twilight Zone or a science fiction movie.

There's a popular saying, "thinking outside the box," which

refers to thinking in creative and innovative ways. I'm fond of calling what you're about to discover "dynamiting the box."

Why?

Because it's that different from what's typically taught about emotions and happiness – even the most creative and innovative of teachings.

As you read, you may feel at times overwhelmed, disoriented, skeptical, or uncomfortable.

You may be aware of thoughts that actively resist, disagree with, or reject what I'm saying.

You may even find yourself getting angry at me, or judging me harshly for a variety of reasons.

All of that is to be expected.

You can't experience True Happiness without a radical shift in your perceptions about yourself, other people, the world, and the beliefs, ideas, and strategies you relied on previously.

Plus, as we both know …

Radical shifts can appear extremely challenging!

No matter how far "out there" what I'm sharing may seem at first (and it may not depending on your background), the journey we're going to take together, and the ultimate destination you'll reach after taking it, are very real – and you *can* "get there from here."

I have a confession to make before we continue our journey together.

When I was first beginning to See and Experience what I'm sharing here, I noted that what I was Seeing and Experiencing was diametrically opposed to what *ALL* the experts were saying about emotions and happiness.

That seemed very strange to me, especially because many of the experts had such extraordinary credentials.

Two questions haunted me at the time:

1. How and why could it be that I'm Seeing and Experiencing something no one else seems to See or Experience?
2. How could I possibly be such a lone voice in the wilderness ... and ... be correct?

As a result, there were many moments when I wondered if I was going crazy. But I simply couldn't deny what I was Seeing and Experiencing.

It was so clear.

It felt so "right."

As time passed, I watched what I was Seeing and Experiencing deepen and come more and more into focus, like focusing a camera until a blurry image becomes sharp and clear.

When I later began to see that other people were having the same True Happiness Experience I had, after discovering what you'll discover in this book, my doubts and fears dissolved, and I simply rested in what I knew to be True.

Next, throughout these pages, as you've already seen, you'll see me capitalize, bold, and sometimes underline the first letters of words. I do that to highlight the gigantic difference between The Truth and the lies, illusions, stories, and myths we've accepted as True, even though they're not.

If you've read any of my other books, or if you read a lot of non-fiction books in general, you'll notice that this book is much shorter than the typical non-fiction book you see on the shelves.

The reason for that is simple.

A book should only contain enough words and pages to get the job done.

No fluff, filler or extraneous detail.

Fewer words were required to get this "job" done.

Finally, in writing this book, all that mattered to me was helping you discover and actually experience True Happiness all the time, no matter what's going on around you.

I therefore allowed my "Inner Renegade" to express itself, and you'll see me break many rules relating to writing, grammar, structure, and style.

You'll see that my writing style is very conversational. I hope you'll actually feel like we're having a private, one-on-one conversation, just the two of us.

This book is about you Experiencing True Happiness, all the time, no matter what's going on around you. It's not about rules, formulas, grammar, or paragraph or sentence structure.

Finally, I want to repeat two things before we continue:

1. Nothing in this book is theory.

2. I really mean Experiencing True Happiness all the time, *no matter what's going on around you.*

I have Experienced and continue to Experience everything I discuss here.

Everything.

To give you four extreme examples (I could share hundreds of others), I've consistently Experienced True Happiness, as it will be defined here, even during:

▷ A two-year bout with "Murphy's Law" where just about everything that could go wrong, did go wrong, in all aspects of my life – the only exception being my relationship with my kids.

▷ A financial crisis during which cash flow dried up, expenses skyrocketed, I was unable to pay my bills, piled up hundreds of thousands of dollars in debt, and didn't know if I'd be able to turn things around or have to go bankrupt (with a wife and two kids to support).

▷ A complicated separation and ultimate divorce from my wife.

▷ Cataract surgery on my left eye where the surgeon made a mistake, damaged my cornea, and left me with "blur spot" in my field of vision that couldn't be corrected

My life has always been the "laboratory" from which springs everything I teach, share and coach.

I'm certain that the Murphy's Law, financial, marriage, and eye dynamics manifested when they did and how they did so I could verify The Truth of what I'm sharing here for myself.

I also believe that's why the Murphy's Law and financial "crises" ultimately resolved themselves, quickly and easily, once they'd served their purpose.

Thousands of other people worldwide are also Experiencing consistent True Happiness after discovering what you're about to discover here, even while having experiences you might call bad, awful, terrible, disastrous, tragic, bad luck, Murphy's Law, failure, etc.

KEY POINT:

Everything I share in this book is real, possible, and do-able, including by YOU!

If you're ready to rock and roll, discover secrets about happiness you've never heard before, have your mind literally blown, and leap through a gateway into a consistent Experience of True Happiness, turn the page to begin your journey.

The Hidden Motivation
For Everything You Do

Imagine, for a moment, that you found a Magic Genie.

You released her from her bottle and she said, "I will grant you three wishes but there's one condition: You must tell me, being very precise, why you want what you wish for."

What would you wish for and what reasons would you give?

Since you can't actually tell me through the pages of this book, I'm going to make something up and express it in the form of a fictional dialog between the Genie and a woman named Annie.

I've taken some creative liberties with the dialog to make an important point.

Genie: "What's your first wish?"

Annie: "For my first wish, I'd like a hundred million dollars cash."

Genie: "*Why* do you want the hundred million dollars?"

Annie: "So I can quit my job, travel the world, and live any way I choose the rest of my life."

Genie: "Why do you want to quit your job, travel the world, and live any way you choose?"

Annie: "What do you mean?"

Genie: "Why do you want those things?"

Annie: "I want that kind of freedom."

Genie: "Why do you want that kind of freedom?"

Annie: "I don't understand the question."

Genie: "If you had that kind of freedom, what would it actually give you, the bottom line?"

Annie: "I'd be happy."

Genie: "I see. So what you really want is to be happy, and you think the hundred million dollars would make that possible. Is that right?"

Annie: "Yes."

Let's look at another example.

Genie: "What's your second wish?"

Annie: "I'd like to lose 35 pounds and stay at that weight, looking fit, healthy, and attractive, no matter what I eat and whether I exercise or not."

Genie: "Why do you want to lose 35 pounds and live and look like that?"

Annie: "I'd look hot."

Genie: "Why do you want to look hot?"

Annie: "I'd feel better about myself when I look in the mirror, and I'd be very attractive to men."

Genie: "Why do you want to feel better about yourself and be very attractive to men?"

Annie: "Because right now I don't like what I see in the mirror and I feel judged by men when they look at my body."

Genie: "So, if you liked what you saw in the mirror and you knew men found you attractive, what would that give you?"

Annie: "I'd be happy."

Genie: "I see. So you don't really want to lose 35 pounds, keep it off, and look fit no matter what. You want to be happy, and you think losing the weight and looking hot would make that possible. Is that correct?"

Annie: "I never thought about it like that before, but yes, that's correct."

I've gone through this exercise with thousands of people in live seminars and the dialog flow is always the same.

It's *always* a feeling the person really wants.

Whatever they *say* they want, the "thing" they'd wish for, is just an imagined pathway into the feeling they really want.

Most importantly, the feeling they always wanted, ultimately, was happiness.

Hmmm.

The examples above are simple. Sometimes I'd have to ask more questions, dig and probe a bit more, but the person would *always* say it was happiness they really wanted.

I never pushed it, forced it, or played mind games.

The person always came to the "happiness conclusion" on their own, naturally.

Go ahead and try it yourself – with anything you'd ask a Magic Genie for right now if you had access to one.

Pick a few things you really want right now. Then keep asking yourself, "Why do I want that?" or "If I got _____, what would it actually give me?"

It's actually quite fascinating to see this in motion for yourself.

Why?

You have a long list of things you want to change, fix, improve, create, or experience in your life. You'd swear on a stack of bibles in a court of law that you really want what's on your list.

But you don't REALLY want what's on your list – more money, a better job, more or better "stuff and things," to be in a relationship if you're alone (or a better relationship if you're in one now), more or better sex, to help others or save the world, lose weight, have something related to the body appear or disappear, etc.

You want to be happy ...

And you too think getting what's on your list will make you happy.

This Truth is buried so deeply that we rarely see it unless a gigantic spotlight is shined on it like I've done here.

Here's the other fascinating thing you See if you look closely ...

> What you *think* will happen when you get
> what's on your list <u>never</u> happens.

Never.

Here's what really happens:

▷ You get something on your list and immediately move on to your next project, want, or goal – without stopping to "smell the roses" or enjoying your victory.

▷ You get something on your list, you do stop to smell the roses, but you don't feel happy when you do it. It actually feels surprisingly empty.

▷ You get something on your list, and you feel a brief flash of happiness, but it disappears quickly as "reality" sets in.

What "reality" sets in?

There are still tons of things on your list you still don't have.

Or something new gets added to your list to replace what you just got.

And the apparent "lack" of having what's still on your list causes you to feel un-happy again.

Almost immediately.

There can be exceptions, of course.

The temporary "getting something you want high" can sometimes last a few days or weeks, but it's rare.

The typical Human Experience consists of an ever-expanding "Wish List" and an endless "assembly line" of unfulfilled wants and desires.

You know what I'm talking about.

You've experienced it.

Over and over.

Yet, you're so mesmerized by the things on your list, and the stories about how happy you'll be when you get them, that you forget or ignore this obvious fact.

We all do.

And we continue on a fruitless quest to be happy by traveling down paths that can't take us into **True Happiness** ...

Until The Truth sets us free

It's kind of like dog racing at the track. The dogs are trained to chase mechanical rabbits. But the thing is, no matter how hard they try, how badly they want it, how strong they are, how fast they run, what they eat, or how luxurious their kennels are, they'll never catch the rabbit.

It's *always* just out of reach – by design.

You could also think of it like a hamster on a wheel – run, run, run, effort, effort, effort, try, try, try – but ultimately getting nowhere.

Happiness is the "rabbit" you've been chasing but never catching.

Trying to get what's on your list is your "wheel."

Nothing will change for you until you ...

GET OFF THE TRACK AND OFF YOUR WHEEL

I'll show you how to do that in the pages of this book.

So ... here's a question I want to drop into your pond and allow to ripple out as you turn the pages of this book.

If what you REALLY want is to be happy, and if you were happy all the time, no matter what was going on around you, how do you think that would change your life ... and ... the content of what's on your list?

It would change, right?

How would it change?

First, your list would shrink ...

Dramatically.

Second, new things would get added to your list that were never on it before.

Very different sorts of things.

Third, you wouldn't be as mesmerized and obsessed by getting what's on your list. Things would seriously mellow out for you.

On and on it goes.

More on this later.

I've got to add that it's not just that happiness is the hidden motivation behind everything on your list.

There's more.

It goes deeper.

Let me explain it to you this way.

You have your routine, what you do Monday through Friday, nine to five.

Maybe for you it's a job, being a parent, a student, or a volunteer of some kind.

You spend the biggest chunk of your time following your routine.

But then you carve out chunks of time (and maybe daydream about the day when you can carve out bigger chunks) to do other things like play sports, watch sports, paint or sculpt, write, read novels, watch movies or plays or TV shows – what

I call "opportunities to play, explore, and express yourself creatively."

We often call those opportunities fun, passions, and hobbies.

The examples I've shared are just a small sample of what's possible for you when you deviate from your daily routine.

Now here's the fascinating thing few people realize. To explain it, I'm only going to discuss reading novels, watching movies, and watching sporting events, although the same dynamics apply to any hobby, passion, or other thing you do for fun, to play, explore, or express yourself creatively.

If you love reading great novels, why do you love it?

What does it give you?

If you love watching great movies, why do you love it?

What does it give you?

If you love watching sporting events, why do you love it?

What does it give you?

If you take the time to look closely and examine what you see, you'll see that reading great novels, watching movies and sporting events is all about what I call "inner experiences."

If you read a great novel, a lot happens as you turn the pages. People say things, do things, and talk to each other. But that's not what you really care about. What you really care about is the FEELINGS you experience as the story unfolds.

If you watch a great movie, a lot happens as the minutes pass. People say things, do things, talk to each other, and you see amazing special effects. But that's not what you really care about. What you really care about is the FEELINGS you experience as the story unfolds.

If you watch sporting events, a lot happens. Quarterbacks pass and running backs run in American football. Goals get scored in soccer. Forehands, backhands, and lobs get hit in tennis. There are beautiful drives and putts in golf. But that's not what you really care about. What you really care about is the FEELINGS you experience while all the action takes place.

What you read in novels, see on the screen in movies, and see your sports heroes do on fields, courts, and courses is just the trigger or "on switch" for the FEELINGS you really want to experience inside yourself.

It's *ALL* about the feelings!

A wide variety of feelings.

Take the feelings away, and ALL the fun and pleasure you get from reading novels, watching movies and sporting events, and everything else you do to play, explore, and express yourself creatively – EVERYTHING – disappears with them.

Hmmm.

So, the hidden motivation for getting everything on your list of what you want to change, fix, improve, create, or experience in your life is feeling … happiness.

And, the hidden motivation for all the things you do to play, explore, and express yourself creatively is to experience a wide variety of FEELINGS.

Hmmm.

Keep this in mind as you turn the page to continue your journey …

CHAPTER

2

The Big Problem

As it relates to happiness, "The Big Problem" has six parts.

The first part of The Big Problem:

You want to be happy, but you're not … consistently or at all.

The second part of The Big Problem:

You've tried all kinds of ways to be happy.

Odds are, you've tried changing things "out there" in the world, what I call "Story Space."

Story space is where all the people are, all the places are, all the things and objects are. Story Space is also where your body appears to be.

Odds are, in your quest to be happy by changing details in Story Space, you've changed jobs or climbed the corporate ladder.

You've changed relationships.

You've changed your diet and exercise routine.

You've moved into different homes or apartments.

You've purchased different clothes and cars.

You've increased your income or net worth.

You've achieved many "goals."

Odds are, you've tried changing things "in here," meaning inside of you, what I call "Inner Space."

Inner space, as the name would suggest, is a space that appears to exist inside of you. You can't see it. You can't touch it. Nobody else can see it. Nobody else can touch it. But it's perceived as a vast space inside of you.

Thoughts, emotions, feelings, and bodily sensations appear in Inner Space.

Odds are, in your quest to be happy by changing details in Inner Space, you've tried physical, emotional, energetic, or spiritual healing modalities.

Odds are, you've tried to delete, change or "reframe" the content of Inner Space using various techniques.

Odds are, everything failed, or you wouldn't be here – just like everything failed for me until I discovered and Experienced the big breakthrough being documented here.

KEY POINT:

> Happiness is the most elusive desire in The Human Experience.

The third part of The Big Problem:

You do feel happy sometimes, but it never lasts, and no one has ever given you a surefire recipe for getting it back when it disappears.

The fourth part of The Big Problem:

Even if you appear to feel happy from time to time, or even for a lot of the time in phases, what's being experienced is generally a pale, pale, pale imitation of how happy you can actually BE … all the time.

You may not be consciously aware of this part of the problem, but you'll see what I mean and really "get it" if you leap through the portal I'm opening for you through this book.

The fifth part of The Big Problem:

Other people appear to be happy and that makes you feel worse in contrast.

However, as the old saying goes, "Looks can be deceiving."

The Truth is, most people who appear to be happy aren't as happy as they appear to be. It's an act, a cleverly crafted mask that obscures how they're actually feeling most of the time.

Or, as I explained above, even if they *are* as happy as they appear to be, what's being experienced is a pale, pale, pale imitation of how happy they can actually BE … all the time.

The sixth and perhaps largest part of The Big Problem:

What is happiness anyway?

If you're brutally honest with yourself, you'll see that you don't really know.

The definition of "happy" is usually blurry and fuzzy or inaccurate.

It seems like you know – like it's what I call "Duh obvious" – but it isn't.

Why don't we know?

Because if you're like I used to be, and like so many folks I chat with, you've never taken a really close look or carefully examined the question, "What is happiness?"

How can you hit a target if you don't know what it is?

You can't.

We'll be taking a close look at the question in the chapters that follow, and my guess is, you'll be quite surprised, maybe even shocked, by what you see.

It's now time to take a look at the popular and accepted perspectives on emotions and happiness, and the common "prescriptions" offered for how to be happy.

Once we do that, you'll be ready to discover The Big Solution.

Continue your journey on the next page.

CHAPTER
3

Lies, Illusions, And Stories

The primary reason you're not experiencing True Happiness on a consistent basis right now is that you've accepted a series of lies, illusions, and stories as True.

Let's examine those lies, illusions, and stories now.

There are numerous experts on the subject of happiness. When I use the word "expert" here, I'm referring to:

— Doctors

— Psychiatrists

— Psychologists

— Authors and speakers

— Coaches and Practitioners

— Healers

— Anyone else who claims to have expertise on helping you be happy

The language differs, but the messages shared by experts contain the same seven core **<u>assumptions</u>** that are either stated directly or implied:

1. There are "positive" emotions, like happiness, serenity, excitement, and joy.

2. There are "negative" emotions, like sadness, anger, fear, worry, frustration, and depression.

3. The positive emotions are good, pleasurable, and we want to feel them.

4. The negative emotions are bad, painful, and we don't want to feel them. They're also "toxic," harmful, can cause damage of various kinds (including illness), and can block your spiritual or personal development.

5. We're "at war" with our negative emotions.

6. We must therefore take action to manage, minimize, muffle, reframe, ignore, release, dissolve, destroy, transmute, heal core causes, or eliminate negative emotions.

7. If we're successful with the actions taken in assumption 6, we'll win the war and be happy.

I used the word "assumptions" above, and I intentionally bolded and underlined it.

Why?

Because while most people would say it's "Duh ... obvious" that all seven assumptions above are accurate and true ...

They're not!

They're ALL nothing but extremely seductive lies, illusions, and stories.

They're ALL the result of what you might call a cleverly

crafted mind game or mental "magic trick."

Here's The Truth:

1. There's no such thing as "positive" emotions (except in a story).

2. There's no such thing as "negative" emotions (except in a story).

3. Emotions are not good or bad, pleasurable or painful, harmful, damaging, or helpful (except in a story).

4. Emotions just "are."

5. There's no need to be "at war" with your emotions.

6. ALL emotions can be welcomed and appreciated exactly as they are.

7. There's no need to manage, minimize, muffle, reframe, ignore, release, dissolve, destroy, transmute, heal core causes, or eliminate certain emotions – while retaining others.

KEY POINT:

> The path to True Happiness looks nothing like what you've been taught and accepted as true.

That's a big, bold claim, right?

Sure it is.

But I don't expect you to take my word for it.

No, no, no.

I'm going to pull back the curtain, show you how the mind game is played, how the mental magic trick is done, and give you the opportunity to prove *everything* I share to yourself – beyond the shadow of any doubt.

I'll help you exchange lies, illusions, and stories for a direct and consistent experience of Truth.

After laying out the seven assumptions just shared, some experts will give you advice and body-centric techniques for "dealing" with negative emotions and managing "stress" – techniques like relaxation, biofeedback, meditation, yoga, exercise, or breathing.

Other experts will tell you about chemicals and the brain, and how you can feel better by taking various supplements or drugs to alter your biochemistry. Many books have been written on this topic.

For our purposes here, I'm not interested in stories about what may or may not happen in your brain.

I'm only interested in what you can actually observe in your own personal experience – and how those observations and experiences can shift when The Truth is Seen and Experienced.

Other expert advice is more mentally oriented and tells you to simply:

▷ Keep your focus in the present moment (problems only exist when you focus on the past or future)

▷ Have compassion for everyone and everything, including yourself, and you'll be happy

▷ Realize we're all "One"

▷ Practice "mindfulness"

▷ Have an attitude of gratitude

▷ Stop to smell the roses in your life

▷ Release your attachment to outcomes

▷ Accept everything that happens without judgment

▷ Visualize images, colors, or other appearances in your mind ("Inner Space")

On and on ...

When I was given these mental suggestions in my younger years, it used to make me really mad.

Why?

Because while I could often see The Truth in what the experts were saying, either they didn't tell me *how* to do what they were recommending, or what they told me to do didn't work.

Can you relate?

Finally, there are a variety of "alternative healing techniques" designed and offered by experts to help you become happier. The techniques often involve energy work, tapping, moving the eyes in specific patterns, hypnosis, past life regression, and so on.

Each of the techniques, prescriptions, and recommendations I just shared can *appear* to make you feel better. The literature abounds with testimonials and success stories.

The experts who provide them are generally people who have huge hearts, really care, and really want to help people.

However, for our purposes here, the opportunity is to See – really See – how and why none of the common prescriptions and techniques can take you into the Experience of True Happiness.

Why?

Because every one of them is based on the core assumption that negative emotions actually exist, they're actually bad and damaging, and we really do need to get rid of them.

And …

That's simply not True.

I've got to get a bit heavy handed now to make an important point.

But before I do, let me make it clear that I have no judgment or criticism of the experts, what they share or recommend.

What I'm about to share is <u>not</u> an attack on or a criticism of anyone or anything.

I'm simply shining the light of Truth onto lies, illusions, and stories.

Here are some key questions to ask yourself right now, then take a brutally honest look at the answers you find.

First, is the world Truly a happier place as a result of all of the expert advice, the books, the seminars, the videos, the audios, the tools, the techniques, and the therapies?

Brutally honest answer:

No!

Second, are *you* truly happy after doing what you've done?

Brutally honest answer:

No!

Third, if you can say, "I'm happ*ier* than I used to be," I'll expand the question to: Are you as happy as you know *you can be* after all you've done?

Brutally honest answer:

No!

If you think any of these answers is "Yes," you'll likely realize it's actually "No!" after finishing this book.

I'm here to tell you that the world won't get happier, and you won't get happier, or become as Truly Happy as you can be, unless a huge, and I mean HUGE change is made.

I'm going to show you how to make that HUGE change.

Here's the unexamined fantasy most of us hold, whether we're consciously aware of it or not:

1. Negative emotions will disappear.

2. Positive emotions will remain.

3. When I only experience positive emotions, I'll be happy (or experience bliss, ecstasy, nirvana, etc.).

I'm here to tell you that the unexamined fantasy will <u>never</u> become reality.

I'm going to show you why that's true, and how you can go beyond the fantasy to Experience True Happiness, all the time, no matter what's going on around you.

What is True Happiness?

Historically, that has been "The Big Mystery," but in the next chapter, we'll solve it.

Turn the page to continue your journey.

CHAPTER

4

The Big Mystery

You experience emotions.

Every day.

All day.

As you perceive it now, you enjoy some and struggle with others.

Every day.

All day.

Emotion is a HUGE part of The Human Experience.

As I explained in Chapter 1, happiness is the hidden motivation behind virtually everything you do.

Feelings are the hidden motivation behind everything you do to play, explore, and express yourself creatively.

But what are feelings?

What is "happiness"?

Truth be told, it has always been a big mystery.

By the way, from this moment on, even though emotions and feelings are synonyms for the same thing, I'll just be using the word "emotion" for the singular and "emotions" for the plural.

Given how prominent emotion is in our lives, and how vital happiness is to us, it amazes me that most people (including me for the first 46 years of my life) never take the time to ask about or examine what emotions really are in general, and what "happiness" is in specific.

It's like emotions are so obvious, so in our faces, that it seems there's no reason or need to examine what they actually are.

But there *is* a reason ...

There *is* a need ...

If you want to be **Truly Happy**.

So, let's take a look now.

We'll first look at emotion in general, then move on to happiness in specific.

As you read this chapter and the one that follows, you may feel they're overly complex, technical, or "heady."

You may not feel that way.

If you do, and you invest the time and effort to get clear on what's being shared (even if it involves re-reading the chapters several times), I promise it will become crystal clear.

I'll also say that crystal clarity on these dynamics is what opens the door to experiencing True Happiness on a consistent basis.

KEY POINT:

> The emphasis here is ALWAYS on what you actually ob-
> serve in your own personal, direct experience – not ideas,
> concepts, or theories.

If you close your eyes and "look" at what I've called Inner Space, what do you see?

If you're able to See what's really there, what you See is a vast space with no beginning and no end. No boundaries.

There's the hint of an up-down, front-back, right-left in Inner Space, but if you look closely, the space is so infinite in scope that those terms don't have much meaning.

Inner Space is always there and never changes.

It doesn't move.

It's just there.

Still and quiet you could say.

In this way, Inner Space could be compared to a movie screen. People, places, things, images, and colors appear and move on movie screens, but the screen itself never changes, never moves. The screen is not the person, place, thing, color, or image that appears on it.

Just like people, places, things, images, and colors can appear and move on movie screens, you can observe three appearances and movements in Inner Space:

1. Thoughts

2. Emotions

3. Bodily Sensations

For our purposes here, you must ask yourself, what is it that appears in Inner Space that I call "emotions?"

Truth is, it's impossible to define what emotions are precisely, but if you look closely, you'll notice that emotions are *something* that appear in Inner Space, apparently out of nowhere, and seem to flow, move, or vibrate.

For purposes of discussion, let's name that *something* that appears to flow or move or vibrate "energy."

So, for our purposes here, and for simplicity, let's define emotions as "the movement of energy in Inner Space."

There are times when the movement of energy appears slow.

There are times when the movement of energy appears faster.

There are times when the movement of energy appears to be very fast.

There are times when the movement of energy is so fast and strong, it feels like an emotional hurricane or tornado is swirling in Inner Space.

The speed of movement isn't all we see if we look closely at emotion, however.

There's something else there.

Within the movement itself, whether it's slow, fast, very fast, or storm-like, there's an infinite variety of expressions or "signatures" that are unique and distinct.

If I were to ask you if anger feels different from happiness, or if sadness feels different from excitement, or if depression feels different from embarrassment, or if love feels different from hate, you'd say, "Yes, they *FEEL* different."

For our purposes here, and for simplicity, let's define the

unique and distinct variety of emotional signatures as vibrating at certain "frequencies."

So far, our examination has revealed that what we call emotion is a combination of movement, speed, and frequency – all appearing in the vastness of Inner Space.

In this way, you could compare the movement of energy in Inner Space to a radio station, and the speed and frequency of the movement to music.

You tune your radio dial to a certain frequency and you hear rock music. You tune the dial to another frequency and you hear pop, classical, jazz, or new age music. Each type of music has its own unique signature that's easily recognizable.

The energy in Inner Space begins to move, and the speed and frequency changes in response to what happens to us:

▷ Someone says something critical about you, the energy moves in a specific way and gets tuned to a specific frequency.

▷ Someone compliments you, the energy moves in a different way and gets tuned to a different frequency.

▷ Someone's car smashes into yours in a parking lot, the energy moves in another way and gets tuned to a different frequency.

▷ You get an unexpected big bonus check at work, the energy moves in a different way and gets tuned to a different frequency.

▷ Your partner leaves you, the energy moves in a different way and gets tuned to a different frequency.

You get the idea.

To summarize what you've discovered so far, here's what happens in your actual experience – every day, all day:

1. Something happens in the world ("Story Space").

2. The energy in Inner Space begins to move in specific ways in response to what happened.

3. As the energy moves, it gets tuned to a specific frequency.

4. Steps 2 and 3 repeat as new things happen to you.

5. You experience differing emotions as a result.

Even though the movements and frequencies of energy in Inner Space have an infinite variety of expressions, we don't have an infinite number of words to describe them.

But we do have a lot of words to describe them.

A friend of mine, Dr. John Demartini, once told me he went through the dictionary to research the number of words in the English language used to describe emotions. He said he found nearly four thousand words.

Here's a question for you …

When you observe energy moving in a specific way and at the specific frequencies you call anger, fear, frustration, sadness, depression, excitement, happiness, or peace, how do you know that's what it is?

How do you KNOW you're feeling anger, fear, frustration, sadness, depression, excitement, happiness, or peace?

There was a time in your life, during childhood, when you were aware of the movements and frequencies of energy in Inner Space, but you didn't have words for them.

You had no idea what anger, fear, frustration, sadness, depression, excitement, happiness, or peace were.

It was all just "movements of energy" to you at that time.

Hmmm.

Like everything else in life, you had to *learn* to link specific movements and frequencies of energy to specific names.

You'd say that "negative" emotions like anger, fear, frustration, sadness, and depression feel "bad."

But here's the thing …

How do you KNOW they feel "bad?"

There was a time in your life, during childhood, when you were aware of the movements and frequencies of energy in Inner Space, but you had no reference points of "good" or "bad" for them.

They were just "neutral" movements and frequencies of energy to you, for lack of a better term.

Hmmm.

Like everything else in life, you had to *learn* to judge certain frequencies as good and bad, pleasant and painful, feel good and feel bad.

There are people who would disagree with me on this. There are people who would insist that babies somehow know that certain feelings and sensations are painful and that's why they cry.

From my perspective, there's no way to know what the inner experience of a baby actually is, and I stand by what I just shared, speaking from actual Experience, not speculation.

Based on what you now know:

▷ When you say, "I'm frustrated," what are you really saying?

▷ When you say, "I'm depressed," what are you really saying?

▷ When you say, "I'm sad," what are you really saying?

▷ When you say, "I'm bored," what are you really saying?

▷ When you say, "I'm afraid," what are you really saying?

▷ When you say, "I'm stressed out," what are you really saying?

▷ When you say, "I'm excited," what are you really saying?

▷ When you say, "I'm at peace," what are you really saying?

▷ When you say, "I'm happy," what are you really saying?

All you're *really* saying is ...

"I'm aware of emotional energy moving in Inner Space in a specific way and vibrating at a specific frequency that I'm *calling* _____" [fill in the blank with the name of an emotion].

KEY POINT:

> What most people call "happiness" is just one of the frequencies the movement of energy in Inner Space can be tuned to.

Based on what I just shared, I must now ask you this ...

When you say "I want to be happy," what do you really want?

Are you saying you only want to experience one frequency of emotion, all day, every day?

In certain spiritual or metaphysical circles, the answer to that question would be "Yes," and the name for the one frequency would be bliss, ecstasy, or nirvana.

But I'm here to tell you the answer is "No!"

That's why I explained about how important emotions, *a wide variety of emotions*, are to your enjoyment of novels, movies, and sporting events, play, exploration, and creative expression.

KEY POINT:

Feeling only one frequency of emotion in life would be boring and would cheat you out of much of the richness of what I call "The Human Story."

Experiencing a "flatline" of bliss, ecstasy, or nirvana is a nice story, a nice fantasy, especially when we feel so unhappy so much of the time, but it's not The Truth as I've Experienced it.

"Okay, Robert," you might say, "I hear you. I get your point. I wouldn't want to limit my experience to just one frequency, but I would want to limit it to only the *positive* frequencies."

I know how logical that seems.

How right it seems.

But I must say to you …

That's <u>not</u> what you REALLY want.

You don't want to limit your emotional Experience at all.

KEY POINT:

True Happiness is <u>not</u> about experiencing a limited number of emotions. It's about Experiencing the full range of emotional movements and frequencies in all their glory.

True Happiness is about Experiencing the full range of movements and frequencies ... without ... names or judgments of positive-negative, good-bad, pleasurable-painful, feel good-feel bad.

Does that sound logical or interesting but impossible or "pie in the sky" to you?

If so, consider this ...

You've already experienced True Happiness many times without realizing it.

I'll give you four examples, although you'll find many more in your memory banks.

Example 1: Riding A Roller Coaster

When you ride a roller coaster (or any high-speed ride at an amusement park) – if you enjoy that sort of experience – you experience many emotions.

They whiz by very quickly.

But in that context – a ride that's meant to be fun – you don't stop the flow of emotions to name what's appearing. You don't constantly narrate to yourself, "This is fear, this is adrenaline rush, this is excitement."

Similarly, with some exceptions, you don't stop to judge the emotions either. You don't say "this feels good, this feels bad."

You just FEEL!

And you love "just FEELING."

The emotions just whiz by quickly, without names, descriptions, or judgments.

All the emotions just blend together into one experience that you perceive as "pleasurable."

In general.

There can always be exceptions.

That's True Happiness!

Would you rather feel only one emotion or a limited range of emotions while riding the roller coaster?

Nope. No way.

You'd stop going to amusement parks if the rides were "flat" experiences like that.

Example 2: Reading a Great Novel

When you read a great novel, and you're really into the story, you experience many emotions. Like riding the roller coaster, those emotions whiz by as you turn the pages.

You're aware of them all, but you don't label them, describe them, or judge them.

You just FEEL …

And you love "just FEELING."

In general.

There can always be exceptions.

That's True Happiness!

Would you rather feel only one emotion or a limited range of emotions while reading novels?

Nope. No way.

You'd stop reading novels if it was a "flat" experience like that.

Example 3: Watching a Great Movie

When you watch a great movie, you experience many emotions as the story unfolds. Like riding the roller coaster and reading the great novel, those emotions simply whiz by as the minutes pass.

You're aware of them all, but you don't label them, describe them, or judge them.

You just FEEL ...

And you love "just FEELING."

In general.

There can always be exceptions.

That's **True Happiness!**

Would you rather feel only one emotion or a limited range of emotions while watching movies?

Nope. No way.

You'd stop going to movies if they were "flat" experiences like that.

Example 4: If You're A Phase 2 Player

If you're a Phase 2 Player (meaning you're aware of my *Busting Loose* and Phase 2 work), you've been actively applying The Teachings and using the tools, virtually every time you've applied the tool called "The Process," you've experienced a moment, maybe longer, where you experienced the emotion called "discomfort" without a name, description, or judgment.

That's **True Happiness!**

If you've been playing the Phase 2 Game a long time, you've therefore had the experience of **True Happiness** hundreds, maybe thousands of times without realizing it.

Okay. Now we've gotta go back to something I shared in the previous chapter.

Imagine for a moment that you're riding a roller coaster and enjoying it, or you're reading a great novel and you're really into it, or you're watching a great movie and you're really caught up in the action.

If you were doing that, and you were able to freeze the flow of emotions, sort them, label and judge them as positive and negative (according to traditional definitions), you *would* judge many of them as "negative."

However, as we've already established, in your actual experience, those "negatives" are actually merged with and perceived as "positives."

Hmmm.

And let me ask you this ...

While you're riding a roller coaster and enjoying it, reading a great novel you're really into, or watching a great movie you're really caught up in, can you see any reason why what you're feeling is "toxic" or "bad" or "harmful" or "damaging?"

Nope.

Can you see any reason why what you're feeling would limit your personal or spiritual development?

Nope.

Hmmm.

We'll be discussing all of this in greater detail in the next chapter, but for now, it's important to have this form of clarity and foundation to build from.

Turn the page to discover the "magic trick" that was used to transform the diverse movements and frequencies of energy in Inner Space into the "positive" emotions we enjoy and welcome, and into the "negative" emotions we dislike and reject.

CHAPTER
5

The Mind Machine

If there's no such thing as positive and negative emotions, pleasurable or painful emotions, helpful and damaging emotions, feel-good or feel-bad emotions, but it seems like there is, something must be creating the illusion of positive and negative, pleasure and pain, helpful and harmful.

That "something" is what I call "The Mind Machine."

Depending on your awareness of traditional definitions, you may think what I'm calling "The Mind Machine" is the same as what's usually called the subconscious mind, unconscious mind, or ego.

In some ways, those comparisons are accurate. But in many other ways, as you'll see, they're not.

KEY POINT:

You're invited to simply look at The Mind Machine in the way I depict it here, and resist the temptation to compare it or cobble it together with other ideas and concepts like subconscious, unconscious, ego, etc.

In this chapter, we'll be looking at what The Mind Machine is, how it works, and how it actually makes the illusion of positive and negative emotions appear real.

KEY POINT:

It is important to look at everything I share about The Mind Machine as a metaphor, a model designed to point to something that's impossible to define precisely with words, ideas, and concepts.

The metaphors and model I'm using are very accurate and extremely supportive, but they're still just metaphors and models. You can argue with them, poke holes in them, debate them, and "break" them if you want, but I invite you to resist any temptation that arises to do so.

I could write an entire book on The Mind Machine alone, maybe more than one book, but I'm keeping this description brief and focused for our purposes here.

All machines, including computers, operate according to rules, programs, and formulas.

Take the Google search engine for example.

The Google search engine sits quietly and waits for you to visit and type in a search phrase. When you do, it observes what you typed in, buzzes and whirrs, searches its database, runs specific programs, applies specific formulas ("algorithms"), and search results pop up on the screen.

> Input ... buzz-whirr ... output ... lightning
> fast ... mechanical and machine-like ...

Of course, the quality of the results Google returns is totally dependent on the quantity and quality of what's stored in its database, the nature of the programs it runs, and the specifics contained within its algorithms.

If you type something into Google that it doesn't recognize, it'll still buzz and whirr and pop out results, but they won't help you. Remember this, as it becomes important later.

The Google database was built, and continues to grow, based on what's happening in the Internet-based "world."

As things happen on the Internet, Google finds out about them and adds new entries to its database, filing and classifying them according to its programs and algorithms.

The folks at Google are obsessed with providing the most accurate results possible, so they change the programs and algorithms frequently in an effort to constantly improve.

The Mind Machine works the same way.

The Mind Machine has been observing your life, adding to its database, creating and storing rules and formulas, and modifying programs and algorithms since you were born.

Like Google, The Mind Machine sits quietly waiting for something to appear in Inner Space or Story Space.

When something appears, The Mind Machine, like Google, buzzes, whirrs, searches its database, runs its programs, applies its algorithms, and out pops a "result" that you become aware of.

Input ... buzz-whirr ... output ... lightning
fast ... mechanical and machine-like ...

However, with The Mind Machine, the "result" is a STORY about what was observed in Inner Space or Story Space – a STORY that's told with thoughts, emotions, and sensations.

For purposes of discussion here, imagine that when The Mind Machine buzzes and whirrs after observing something in Inner Space or Story Space, a program runs that attempts to answer three questions:

1. What is this?

2. What does it mean?

3. How should I respond?

To answer the questions – just like Google – The Mind Machine searches its database for "relevant" entries. If it finds relevant entries – again just like Google – it analyzes them in an attempt to find the "best" answers.

All your life, The Mind Machine has been:

▷ Observing appearances in Inner Space and Story Space

▷ Asking the three questions

▷ Answering the three questions based on the information stored in its database and the programs and algorithms that process the information

▷ Storing ALL the appearances and results in its ever-expanding database

▷ Refining its programs and algorithms to get more and more efficient

▷ Putting as much of the buzz-whirr-output on autopilot as possible

KEY POINT:

If you resonate with what I share in this book, you'll have the opportunity and ability to slow the activity in Inner Space enough to see The Mind Machine in motion.

To do its job, The Mind Machine must:

▷ Break everything it observes into pieces

▷ Label the pieces with words

▷ Build stories about the pieces

▷ Store the pieces, words, and stories in its database

For example, when The Mind Machine observes objects in Story Space, it separates and labels them as chairs, cars, trees, mountains, people, etc.

When it observes emotions in Inner Space, it separates them and labels them as anger, fear, frustration, depression, happiness, excitement, and peace.

As you grow up, The Mind Machine "learns."

It catalogs everything it observes and stores the catalog in its database. Then, whenever it observes something that's already in its database, it can answer the three questions at lightning-fast speed.

When The Mind Machine doesn't recognize what it observes, the response time can be much slower – and like Google – the results aren't always accurate or helpful.

The cataloging process continues throughout your life as The Mind Machine encounters more and more appearances that aren't in its database.

Therefore, at this point in your life, because so many movements and frequencies of energy appearing in Inner Space have been cataloged by The Mind Machine, when a specific one appears, and The Mind Machine asks the first question, "What is this?" it finds a match at lightning fast speed, and outputs the name of the emotion when it tells you its story.

To answer the second question, "What does this mean?" The Mind Machine must search its database, looking for past references or past stories to determine the significance or importance of what has been observed.

When The Mind Machine asks "What does this mean?" about people, places, things, or events in Story Space, it's more complicated. But when it asks that question about emotions, it's very simple.

When The Mind Machine asks "What does this mean?" about emotions, it's looking for data on the positive-negative, pleasurable-painful, helpful-harmful judgmental dynamic.

Just like it can output the name of an emotion at lightning-fast speed, The Mind Machine can also output the positive-negative, pleasurable-painful, helpful-harmful judgment at lightning-fast speed.

Story Space Event → Emotion Appears →
"This is anger" → "This feels bad."

buzz-whirr ... lightning fast ... mechanical and machine-like ...

Just like Google.

Really.

You then become aware of the output, accept it as true and accurate, and believe you're actually feeling anger, fear, frustration, or depression (and feeling really "bad"), or actually feeling happiness, excitement, and peace (and feeling really "good").

Except you're not.

It's just a story.

An illusion.

A mental "magic trick."

Now here's the really fascinating thing ...

There's nothing in the emotional movement or frequency of energy itself, what I call the "pure, raw experience," that actually says, "This is anger. This is depression. This is frustration. This is happiness. This is peace. This is serenity."

There's nothing in the movement or frequency of energy itself, the pure, raw experience that tells you it's bad, unpleasant, or harmful if we're speaking about "negative" emotions.

The pure, raw emotional experience is just what it is – a movement and frequency of energy –not good or bad or pleasurable or painful.

Now, obviously, the flip side of that is also true.

There's nothing in the pure, raw emotional experience that says the movement or frequency is good or pleasurable.

All the names and judgments are merely what I'm fond of calling "big lies, illusions, and stories kicked out by The Mind Machine."

To answer the final question, "How should I respond?" The Mind Machine must again search its database, guided by the meaning it assigned when it answered the second question.

It will search all the records in its database, everything that happened to you in the past, what you've learned, all the conclusions that were drawn from those experiences, all the rules and formulas that were created for how to live life, succeed, stay safe, etc.

An action will then be chosen and you'll notice yourself taking it. As you might imagine, there's an infinite variety of responses that can appear as this process completes.

Then, after the buzz-whirr analysis has been completed, new things appear in Inner Space and Story Space, and the three-question process repeats itself endlessly.

When The Mind Machine is in "learning mode" as you're growing up, your responses to the observation of specific movements and frequencies of energy in Inner Space are inconsistent.

As you get older, however, after a lot of data has been processed by The Mind Machine, specific programs and algorithms get created and are locked into place.

After that, anytime The Mine Machine observes a movement of energy it already has in its database, it'll buzz and whir and say, "Oh, I know what that is. That's anger, and that's bad. Oh, I know what that is. That's peace, and that's good. I know what that is. That's happy, and that's good."

From that moment on, The Mind Machine assigns the same labels and meanings and responds the same way – over and over on autopilot, and so quickly that we don't even notice it happening.

Once these dynamics lock into place, we conveniently forget that, through the buzz-whirr of The Mind Machine, *we* broke the movements and frequencies into pieces, *we* named the pieces, *we* judged the pieces, and *we* accepted the lies, illusions, and stories about the pieces as true.

KEY POINT:

As long as you believe there really are positive and negative emotions, the positives are good, the negatives are bad, and happiness is one of the positives, you'll <u>never</u> be Truly Happy.

Never.

Why?

As long as there's a program in The Mind Machine that splits emotions into positive and negative, The Mind Machine will always buzz and whirr, create the split, and while you'll tell yourself you're happy when you feel the positives, there will ALWAYS be negatives you'll try to avoid.

KEY POINT:

The fact that the pure, raw experience of emotion is "neutral" isn't an idea or a concept. It's what you actually <u>Experience</u> when you Experience The Truth.

Part of the magic trick I just described involves two "elements" being bonded together so tightly you can no longer tell they're separate things:

1. The movement and frequency of energy itself – the pure, raw experience

2. The Mind Machine's judgmental story about the pure, raw experience

To help you really get and integrate what I mean, I want to share a metaphor with you – the metaphor of water.

When you look at water in an ocean, lake, stream, or glass, you just see "water."

From a chemical perspective, however, it's actually H_2O, which means two molecules of hydrogen and one molecule of oxygen that have been bonded together.

When the two elements bond, they create something new called water.

If you could see the separate molecules of hydrogen and oxygen, they wouldn't look like "water. " They're just molecules. But, when they bond together, all of a sudden they create water. The separate elements of hydrogen and oxygen disappear, and what we experience, in a variety of different ways, is water.

Let's now apply the metaphor to our experience of emotions.

Our emotional experience begins with the appearance in

Inner Space of a movement of energy vibrating at a specific frequency – the pure, raw experience.

Think of the pure, raw experience as if it were one molecule of oxygen.

Then The Mind Machine hijacks the pure, raw emotional experience, names it, judges it, and tells you a story about it.

Think of The Mind Machine name and judgmental story as if they were the two molecules of hydrogen.

The pure, raw experience (oxygen) bonds with The Mind Machine story (hydrogen) and you think you're experiencing specific positive emotions that feel good and specific negative emotions that feel bad ("water").

Going back to the water metaphor, if hydrogen and oxygen remain bonded, it's going to appear like water. If you separate the hydrogen and the oxygen, however, the elements return to their separate states, and the water disappears.

Similarly, if you either separate the pure, raw emotional experience from The Mind Machine's story about it – or better yet, stop the bonding from occurring in the first place, you experience the pure, raw emotional experience on its own, which is ...

True Happiness!

Okay. Let's now look at some specific examples of The Mind Machine in action as it relates to emotions.

I'm going to choose several examples that you may or may not have actually experienced yourself. Whether you've experienced them or not, you'll receive great support from the specifics illustrated.

I'm going to take some creative liberties with the examples to illustrate key points, so don't be concerned if The Mind Machine buzzes and whirrs and tells you the examples are "unrealistic."

The first step is that something happens in Story Space.

For our first example, imagine that a married couple is standing in a kitchen at a party. Imagine the woman notices her male partner staring at an extremely attractive blonde woman with what appears to be something "extra" in his look.

The Mind Machine observes it.

When it asks the first question, "What is this?" the answer is simple: "My partner is staring at an extremely attractive blonde woman."

lightning fast … mechanical and machine-like …

It will then ask the second question: "What does this mean?"

The Mind Machine would likely consider these possibilities as it scans its database:

▷ Has he lost interest in me?

▷ Is he attracted to her?

▷ Are they having an affair?

▷ Will they have an affair?

▷ Am I in danger?

As The Mind Machine scans its database, there are several possible answers to the question. The possibilities and answers will be shaped by what's in the database.

If the marriage is solid, that data would suggest certain possibilities. If the male partner has a history of "straying," or the woman has been suspecting he's been having an affair, that data would suggest other possibilities.

You get the idea.

After The Mind Machines buzzes and whirrs, a meaning will be chosen and assigned.

For our example, let's choose this meaning: "I suspect he may be having an affair."

At that moment when the question is answered, the inner movement of emotional energy will start moving in a certain way and be tuned to a specific frequency.

Part of the tuning process involves the movement of energy expressing itself with a specific speed and "intensity" that influences where it appears on the scale from quiet to active to storm-like.

The intensity will be determined by the buzz-whirr of The Mind Machine based on what's stored in its database, programs, and algorithms.

Then the frequency will be given a name.

Based on what's been catalogued and stored in The Mind Machine, it could be named fear, anger, or jealousy.

The specific name chosen will be determined by the data, programs, and algorithms stored in the Mind Machine – based on past experiences.

For this example, let's go with "jealousy."

Since this story is an "intense" one, meaning you might be in danger of losing your partner, it's likely the frequency will be fast and intense as it appears in Inner Space.

The Mind Machine will observe the intense "jealousy frequency" appearing in Inner Space and make the judgment:

"This feels <u>bad</u>."

The woman would then accept the "jealousy" and "bad" *stories* without questioning them, and she'll really *believe* she's jealous and that she feels bad.

Boom.

The magic trick is complete!

Faster than the blink of an eye.

The meaning assigned to an appearance in Story Space may or may not be an accurate description of what's actually happening.

In this example, the partner may or may not be having an affair, may or may not even have any interest in the blond woman at all.

But it doesn't matter.

The inner movement of energy will still move as it moves.

It will still be tuned to a certain frequency.

It will sill be named and judged.

And you'll still be convinced you're actually feeling what The Mind Machine story says you're feeling.

Truth be told, it's not "jealousy."

It's just a movement and frequency of energy in Inner Space that's been given a name.

Without a story kicked out by The Mind Machine, it doesn't feel "good" or "bad."

It's just what it is.

You could call it "neutral" or "pleasurable," it doesn't really matter.

KEY POINT:

Ultimately, when you experience True Happiness, you'll perceive all movements and frequencies of energy as being welcome and "pleasurable."

The final question, "How should I respond" will then be asked and answered, and a response will ultimately appear in Story Space in the form of an action.

Then the process of asking and answering the three questions will repeat as new things appear in Inner Space and Story Space.

Let's look at another example.

Imagine you're driving your car and The Mind Machine observes another car running a red light and coming toward you at high speed.

The Mind Machine will answer the first question, "What is this?" by saying, "A car is running a red light." and the second question, "What does this mean?" by saying something like "This is dangerous. I'm not safe."

After meaning is assigned, the inner movement of energy will begin to move in a specific way and be tuned to a specific frequency.

Since this story is an "intense" one, meaning you could be killed, it's likely the frequency will be fast and intense as it appears in Inner Space.

The Mind Machine observes that frequency and repeats the same sequence of questions:

"What is this?"

It will search its database for a similar reference. It's likely it will conclude, "This is fear. I'm afraid."

"What does this mean?"

It will search its database for a similar reference. It's likely it will conclude, "Fear is bad and uncomfortable, and I don't like it."

"How should I respond?"

It will search its database for a similar reference. It's likely it will conclude, "I'd better jam on the brakes or swerve to protect myself."

I could go on and on with examples, but I think you get the idea. If you want to watch a video where I share several other detailed examples, visit this page on my website:

http://www.happinessbook.com/video-examples/

It's important at this point to summarize what you've discovered so far:

1. The inner movement of energy moves in a specific way and gets tuned to a specific frequency in response to what's happening in Story Space.

2. That's pure, raw experience.

3. Pure, raw experience never has a name.

4. There's never anything bad or wrong or uncomfortable about pure, raw experience.

5. Pure, raw experience just "is."

6. The Mind Machine observes pure, raw experience.

7. It buzzes and whirrs and kicks out a story with a name and a judgment for the pure, raw experience.

8. We accept the story as true.

KEY POINT:

> Pure, raw experience always appears first in its pure, raw state ... *and then* ... The Mind Machine hijacks it and tells a judgmental story about it.

What do you think would happen if the stories separated from the pure, raw experiences?

What do you think would happen if the Mind Machine hijackings stopped?

What do you think would happen if no name or judgmental story was ever bonded to the pure, raw emotional experience in the first place?

The movement and frequency of emotional energy would continue to move in an infinite variety of ways and get tuned to an infinite variety of frequencies in response to what happens in Story Space.

You'd be aware of all of them.

You'd welcome all of them.

You'd welcome and appreciate all of them.

No names, labels, or judgments.

Just the pure, raw emotional experience, which is …

True Happiness

I mean that literally.

I actually mean you'd experience the full range of movements and frequencies, but no names would ever appear in your mind – no labels, no judgments – just pure, raw, experience.

KEY POINT:

This is precisely how I and many other people worldwide are experiencing emotions right here, right now.

Anger, frustration, sadness, depression, fear, peace, excitement, even "happiness" dissolve and merge into …

True Happiness

All emotions merge into one welcome flow, in an even more extraordinary way than what I illustrated with the examples of roller coaster rides, great novels, and great movies.

This is real.

It's "practical."

It's do-able – by you.

You already "do it" with novels, movies, sporting events, amusement park rides, etc.

Now it's just time to "do it" with EVERYTHING that happens to you.

I'm not talking about intellectual understanding here.

Let's make that point crystal clear.

Simply *understanding* that a judgmental story has been bonded to a pure, raw experience, and that negative and positive emotions don't exist, does you absolutely no good.

That's not what I'm talking about here.

I'm talking about actually Seeing it, actually Experiencing The Truth of it.

Once you See and Experience The Truth, it's "Game Over" over for un-happiness.

Once you See and Experience The Truth, it's "Game Over" over for hamsters on wheels and dogs chasing rabbits on racetracks.

If the secret to Experiencing True Happiness is Experiencing pure, raw emotional experience without the judgmental stories The Mind Machine tells about it, then I guess the zillion dollar question is ...

"How do I do that?"

Turn the page to find out.

CHAPTER

6

The Truth Virus

You're probably familiar with the term "virus" as it applies to the human body and computers.

As it relates to the body, when a "virus" is introduced into the body, it interacts with cells in the body and has a "harmful or corrupting influence" on them. In short, it changes how the cells in the body function.

As it relates to a computer, a virus is a piece of computer code introduced into a computer system that has a detrimental effect – such as corrupting files, deleting files, or destroying data. In short, it changes how the computer functions.

In both cases, one "element" interacts with other "elements" and has a profound impact on them that spreads quickly.

Viruses in the body and on computers are viewed as having negative or damaging impacts.

Here we will discuss a virus that operates in a similar way, but has "positive" or "supportive" impact.

I call it "The Truth Virus."

A virus in the body affects its cells. A virus on a computer affects data, files, and programs.

The Truth Virus affects the database, programs, and algorithms of The Mind Machine.

As you discovered in the previous chapter, the pure, raw experience of emotion always appears first. Then The Mind Machine hijacks it and bonds a judgmental story to it that you become aware of and accept.

The pure, raw experience, True Happiness, is still there.

It hasn't been destroyed or damaged.

It's just bonded to The Mind Machine's judgmental story, like oxygen is bonded to hydrogen in water.

The Truth Virus operates in two stages.

Right now, the database of The Mind Machine contains all sorts of stories about what various emotions are called, which ones are positive, which ones are negative, etc.

In the first stage, The Truth Virus goes into The Mind Machine database and separates the pure, raw experiences from the stories they're bonded to.

In the second stage, The Truth Virus prevents new stories from being bonded to pure, raw experiences going forward.

Viruses in the body and on computers can spread quickly, but they still take time to have full impact.

It's the same with The Truth Virus, although it can take quite a bit longer to work its particular form of magic.

No matter how long it takes, The Truth Virus works its way through the data stored in the Mind Machine database, selectively deleting and altering entries.

The Truth Virus also works its way through the programs and algorithms in The Mind Machine, deleting programs, rewriting programs, installing new programs, and altering algorithms.

You may or may not be aware of it, but this happens with Google all the time, without a virus being involved. The data in the Google database is constantly changing which constantly changes the search results.

In addition, Google changes its programs and algorithms several times a year to ensure that it's delivering the best possible search results, and so savvy Internet marketers or computer programmers can't gain unfair advantages.

The bottom line is that every time the Google database, programs and algorithms change, search results change dramatically too.

It's the same with The Mind Machine.

There are two ways of introducing The Truth Virus into The Mind Machine. I'll discuss the first option in this chapter. The second option, which involves going beyond this book, will be discussed in a later Chapter called "The Red Pill."

It probably won't surprise you to discover that this book contains a strain of The Truth Virus within it, and that The Truth Virus may have *already been introduced* into your Mind Machine.

Up until now, The Mind Machine has been running on its own, on autopilot, performing its magic trick on the flow of emotional energy in Inner Space.

You've been aware of the output, the judgmental story, and you've been experiencing positive and negative emotions as a result.

Up until now, you never took a close look at what was happening.

You never questioned the accuracy of the stories kicked out by The Mind Machine.

So, just by reading this book to this point, two things are happening.

First, the data in The Mind Machine has changed. It now has data that was never there before.

It now contains data that says positive and negative emotions don't exist, that it's all just movements of energy, and an explanation of how The Mind Machine works.

Because The Mind Machine always scans its database when attempting to answer the three questions that drive it, the simple introduction of what you've discovered here so far can create massive changes in how The Mind Machine operates.

I'll be discussing this dynamic in greater detail in a later Chapter called "Jumping The Gap."

Second, as a result of new data being added to The Mind Machine's database, and the continued operation of The Truth Virus, programs and algorithms in The Mind Machine will be added, deleted, and re-written.

Therefore, when The Mind Machine observes things happening in Inner Space and Story Space, it will start answering and responding to the first two questions differently …

**Just because you read this book and had
The Truth Virus introduced into your Mind Machine**

As The Truth Virus does its work, and the content of Inner Space begins to change, two things will happen:

1. The Mind Machine will observe the changes.

2. You will begin to witness the changes.

The double witnessing dynamic will enhance and turbo-charge the impact of The Truth Virus as it continues its work.

As you become more and more aware of what's happening in Inner Space, you'll also begin to actually witness the Mind Machine story separating from the pure, raw emotional experience.

It's a majorly cool Experience, a "great day" when that happens!

Ultimately, the changes in Inner Space will manifest and you'll become aware of them without you "doing" anything, using any sort of technique, practicing, etc.

But to support the process, I'd like to invite you to perform an exercise right now. The exercise has five steps:

Step 1:

I want you to verify, through our own experience, what I've shared so far.

So, in a minute, I want you to put this book down, close your eyes, and become aware of Inner Space.

In this first step, all I want you to do is verify that when you look into Inner Space, you instantly become aware of a gigantic space that has no beginning, no end, no boundaries, no significant up-down, front-back, right-left.

Stop reading right now, perform this first step of the exercise, then pick the book back up and move on to Step 2.

Are you still reading? If so, please stop and perform the first step of the exercise. As I revealed before, if you just read and allow everything I share to swirl at the idea, concept, and intellectual level, you'll miss out on a great gift!

Step 2:

Close your eyes again and observe Inner Space. If you notice emotional energy moving in a certain way, at a specific frequency, witness it and verify that what I said about movement and frequency is accurate from your own personal experience.

If there doesn't appear to be any emotional energy moving, take a moment, think back to a time or imagine a scenario in which you were "very emotional," or take a close look the next time the energy begins to move on its own, and verify that it really does appear as I said it did.

At this point, if you become aware of a movement and frequency of energy, it may be pure, raw experience by itself, or it may be pure, raw experience bonded with a judgmental story.

Either way, just become aware of what's appearing in Inner Space.

Stop reading right now, perform this second part of the exercise, then pick the book back up and move onto Step 3.

Step 3:

If the appearance of emotion in Inner Space is pure, raw experience bonded to a judgmental story, just watch it and see if the story separates from the pure, raw experience. This may happen right away, or it may not happen for a while, until The Truth Virus has had more time to work its magic.

KEY POINT:

You can't force pure, raw experience to separate from the story. There's no technique, strategy, or magic bullet for making it happen. It will happen on its own once The Truth Virus has worked its magic.

Once you've looked into Inner Space, **S**een the pure, raw experience separate from the Mind Machine story, Experienced pure, raw experience, and know that there's nothing bad or unpleasant or painful about it, it's just a movement of energy, it's "Game Over" for un-happiness.

From that moment on, The Truth Virus will continue and ultimately complete its work, but The Mind Machine's "old way" of processing emotions is over forever.

And ...

Your life will never be the same.

Step 4:

You can apply this step as often as you like and I encourage you to do it often.

After you follow the above steps for a while (I can't predict how long), the activity in Inner Space will slow down and you'll be able to see the contents and the buzz-whirr operation of The Mind Machine more easily.

If you're familiar with my previous Teachings and are a Phase 2 Player, you're already an old hat at what I'm about to share as the fourth step.

Next time you're experiencing a movement and frequency of energy in Inner Space you previously called "negative," dive into the middle of it, metaphorically, and do your best to FEEL the pure, raw experience.

I say "dive into" because that's how it felt to me, like I was actually diving into a swirling movement of energy, like diving into the ocean.

The idea is simply to focus on the movement and frequency of energy and fully FEEL what's there.

If you're like me, what you'll discover will blow you away.

What you'll discover is that the pure, raw experience you once called "negative emotion" isn't really all that different from the pure, raw experience you used to call "positive emotion."

It's important to actually Experience this versus simply having an intellectual awareness of the idea and concept I shared with you.

What you'll discover, for example, is that the pure, raw experience named "fear" isn't really all that different from the pure, raw experience named "excitement" – except in a story kicked out by The Mind Machine.

You'll discover, as another example, that the pure, raw experience named "depression" isn't really all that different from the pure, raw experience named "peace of mind" – except in a story kicked out by The Mind Machine.

There may appear to be subtle differences in the pure, raw experiences of what you once called negative and positive emotions.

If you notice any differences, however, they'll be so subtle as to not support the lie, illusion, and story that one feels bad while the other feels good.

If you dive into the pure, raw experience called "depression," for example, you may notice that "depression" feels a bit more slow or heavy or dense than "peace of mind," but the experiences are surprisingly similar, and the sensation of slowness, heaviness, or density doesn't support "depression" feeling really bad while peace of mind feels really good.

If you're someone who has struggled with the movement and frequency of energy in Inner Space called "depression," The Mind Machine may buzz and whirr at this point and kick out a thought that says something like "No, you're wrong, Robert. Depression is different, and it really does feel awful. I hate it."

"No worries," as the Australians say. Once The Truth Virus has completed its work, I guarantee you'll experience The Truth of what I just shared and be able to verify its accuracy for yourself.

At this point, The Mind Machine may be kicking questions like these into Inner Space:

1. If positive and negative emotions are so similar, why do they appear to be so different?

2. How can peace be perceived so positively while depression is perceived so negatively?

The answer is simple: Because the stories kicked out by The Mind Machine are incredibly hypnotic and mesmerizing. If you want to know why that's the case, be sure to read Appendix A called "The Big Why."

It will be a BIG moment in your life when you actually experience The Truth of this.

When that happens, as I explained, you'll move from seeing what's going on (through the "lens" of lies, illusions, and stories) into Seeing what's going on (through the "lens" of Truth).

Step 5:

Observe Inner Space whenever you experience an emotion of any kind, then watch and wait for the story to separate from the pure, raw experience.

At some point, once The Truth Virus makes enough changes in The Mind Machine's database, programs, and algorithms, you'll become aware of the pure, raw experience by itself and actually witness the moment when The Mind Machine comes in, hijacks it, and kicks out its judgmental story – "This is anger. This doesn't feel good. This is frustration. This doesn't feel good. This is excitement. This feels great," etc.

You'll actually See what I just described, that the pure, raw experience always appears first, just as it is, in its pure state, then The Mind Machine grabs hold of it, buzzes, whirrs, gives it a name, and attaches a judgment of good/bad, positive/negative, painful/pleasurable.

Again, I can't predict how quickly this will happen, when, or how.

As I'll explain in the final chapter, you may need to take The Red Pill for The Truth Virus to complete its work in your unique case.

I needed to take The Red Pill on my journey.

What's the net result of The Mind Machine assimilating The Truth Virus?

You've already experienced **True Happiness** when watching movies, reading novels, or riding rides in amusement parks.

What's different in those situations?

The easiest way to explain it is to say that The Mind Machine is very sensitive to the "context" in which things appear in Inner Space and Story Space.

When you read novels or watch movies, The Mind Machine knows what's happening isn't "real" and isn't actually happening to you.

It also knows that the context is play and exploration, so it doesn't engage, doesn't buzz or whirr or bond judgmental stories to the pure, raw experiences appearing in Inner Space.

When you experience amusement park rides, The Mind Machine knows the context is fun and entertainment, so it also doesn't engage, doesn't buzz and whirr and bond judgmental stories to the pure, raw experiences appearing in Inner Space.

However, when it's personal, when something appears to be happening to YOU, when it's therefore "serious" and "important," the context is very different, and The Mind Machine engages, buzzes, whirrs, and performs its positive-negative-emotion magic trick.

Among many other tasks, The Truth Virus transforms the "serious" and "important" context so the Mind Machine doesn't engage in your daily life – just like it doesn't engage when you're on rides at amusement parks, when you're reading novels, or when you're watching movies.

You *can* experience the same dynamic in your daily life that you experience on a roller coaster, watching a movie, reading a novel, all day, every day.

I could go into a lot more detail on what I just shared, but it's not really needed at this point.

So why did I share this?

Because it's possible that The Mind Machine is buzzing and whirring and kicking "doubt thoughts" like these into Inner Space right now for you:

▷ "I just don't see how this could be true."

▷ "No, no, no. Some emotions really do feel bad and others really do feel good."

▷ "This seems impossible."

▷ "This is just some airy-fairy, out-there, woo-woo bullshit."

▷ "I just don't see how I could ever experience fear as good or neutral."

▷ "I just don't see how I could ever experience my depression as good or neutral."

On and on ...

If doubt thoughts like the examples above appear, remember ...

It's just The Mind Machine buzzing, whirring, and kicking thoughts into Inner Space

If The Mind Machine kicks out doubt thoughts like the above examples ... and ... has new data added to its database that shines the light of Truth on them, it accelerates the effectiveness of The Truth Virus!

That's why I shared what I just shared.

As I said, when The Mind Machine observes the content

shared in this book, it'll buzz and whirr and kick thoughts into Inner Space, including various questions.

For a discussion of "frequently asked questions" and my answers, turn the page.

CHAPTER

7

Quieting The Noise

From my experience working with thousands of people around the world, when The Mind Machine observes what I've shared so far, it can buzz and whirr and come up with all sorts of objections, resistance, and arguments about why what I shared isn't true – for you or anyone.

It can also buzz and whirr and come up with an endless list of questions about what has been shared – even if it's accepted.

I call that Mind Machine activity – doubt and endless questioning – "noise."

In this chapter, I'd like to discuss the typical forms of noise The Mind Machine tends to generate as The Truth Virus is introduced and begins doing its work.

I'll do that by sharing a list of common questions I'm asked when sharing this material, and my answers.

I could write an entire book on just questions and answers, but I'll be brief and to the point in this chapter.

The following questions and answers may or may not have crossed your mind, but they represent the questions I'm asked most frequently. Whether they crossed your mind or not, the answers should be supportive to your journey and to The Truth Virus doing its work.

You may notice that some of the answers contain repetitive content. It's therefore possible you'll hear The Mind Machine say something like, "Yeah, yeah, yeah, I know that Robert. You've already said that a million times."

Whether you hear The Mind Machine tell that story or not, the repetition is V-E-R-Y supportive to turbocharging the effectiveness of The Truth Virus.

Q: Isn't it a bit arrogant for you to say that only you know the truth, that everyone else is wrong, and only you are right about emotions and happiness?

A: Everything I share is simply a narrative of what I've seen appear in Inner Space and Story Space, and what I've Experienced in my own life. Through this book, you're invited to look and see if you observe the same things in your own personal experience. "Arrogance" is about having an exaggerated sense of one's own personal importance. None of this is about me personally. It's about you and Truth and True Happiness.

Q: When experiencing something that's not True Happiness, what's the fastest way you've found to shift back to True Happiness quickly?

A: When you ask that question, what you're saying is, "I'm feeling something I don't like. What's the fastest way to change it to something I *do* like." That reinforces the lie, illusion, and story that there really are positive emotions that feel good and negative emotions that feel bad, that we can and should *do something* to get out of the negatives and into the positives.

For the reasons I've shared, that path doesn't lead to True Happiness and I cannot therefore give you a "fastest way" as you request.

If you look deeply into Inner Space and See what's really happening, what has always been happening, your question will dissolve.

I must also share, even though it's a bit off topic, that there's a gigantic myth in the world that says "faster is always better."

Faster is *not* always better.

The best timing for you as a unique individual is always what's "better" if you want to use that word, whether it appears to be fast, slow, or in between.

Q: What are the tricks to sustain a happy state of mind when there isn't enough money in the bank to cover the most basic life expenses?

A: True Happiness is not conditional upon specific things appearing in Story Space, nor is it context-sensitive. It can be your consistent experience, no matter what's going on around you.

There is not one way to be Truly Happy when you have money challenges, another way to be Truly Happy with relationship challenges, and another way to be Truly Happy if you're struggling with an illness.

There's just **True Happiness**, no matter the context.

The only "trick," in any context and with any challenge, is to allow The Truth Virus to complete its work while looking deeply into Inner Space and:

1. **S**eeing what's really going on;

2. **S**eeing the pure, raw experience separate from The Mind Machine story; and

3. Resting in the pure, raw experience.

Q: How do I sustain my sense of humor and joy when The Mind Machine is telling me painful stories?

> **A:** The opportunity here is not to do something to modify what's happening in Inner Space, in this case, to sustain your sense of humor and joy when something else is going on.
>
> The opportunity is to allow The Truth Virus to do enough of its work that you can observe what's appearing in Inner Space and **S**ee what's really happening.
>
> When you're able to do that, the "painful stories" will dissolve and you'll experience **True Happiness**, which you could say includes "humor and joy," although you'd no longer call it by those names.

Q: What about people who take Prozac or other mood-altering drugs? Don't they feel better after taking the drugs?

> **A:** This is actually quite a fascinating question. Before I answer it, I must share that it's likely people who are taking mood altering drugs (perhaps even you if that's why you asked the question) will argue to the death that I'm wrong about this.

But **Truth** is **Truth** when it's **Seen**, and it *can* be **Seen**, even in this context.

For simplicity sake, let's say someone has struggled with depression and is taking a drug to "alleviate" the "symptoms."

Here's what's happens.

1. The Mind Machine learned to call a specific movement and frequency of energy in Inner Space "depression."

2. The Mind Machine made up a story that "depression" is a "feel bad" appearance it wants to get rid of.

3. The drug is taken and a different movement of energy and frequency appears in Inner Space.

4. The Mind Machine observes that new movement and frequency and makes up a story that it's a "feel good" appearance. The person who was feeling "depressed" accepts the story and believes they now feel "better."

5. But that's not **True**.

The "old feeling," *called* depression, wasn't bad, except in a story, and the new "drug feeling" isn't good or better, except in a story.

When we're mesmerized by the stories The Mind Machine tells us, it seems so "Duh … obvious" that certain energy movements and frequencies feel good and others feel bad.

But it's just not **True**.

All appearances are just different movements of energy and frequencies appearing in Inner Space – not good, bad, pleasant, or painful.

I realize how difficult this can be to see and accept … especially if you've struggled with many "feel bad" emotions over long periods of time.

But it's The Truth nevertheless.

Just because a story appears and seems correct doesn't mean it *is* correct.

As I shared, the stories are just learned, mechanical responses – no different than if you typed "depression" into Google and got a bunch of search results saying depression is a bad feeling.

KEY POINT:

You don't need to take my word for any of this. It doesn't matter if you agree, disagree, understand, or don't understand. You can Experience this for yourself once The Truth Virus completes its work.

Q: I'm a parent of two children. My best friend is a parent of three children and one of her children just died. She's in a deep depression and filled with grief. Are you seriously telling me that if one of my children died, I'd be "happy" about it?

A: In a situation like this, it's very unlikely that you'll be able to really "hear" what I have to say here, not right now anyway. The lies, illusions, and stories in The Mind Machine database are too strong and locked in. But I'll share The Truth about this anyway, and what it sets into motion, it sets into motion.

"Grief" and "depression" are names used to describe specific movements and frequencies of energy appearing in Inner Space.

The Mind Machine has bonded a story to those movements and frequencies that says, "This feels really bad."

It's true that *something* higher on the intensity scale is generally appearing in Inner Space when someone *says* they're depressed or feeling grief. But the story that it "feels bad" is simply not True.

When the story separates from the pure, raw experience, it doesn't feel "bad" at all.

Quite the contrary.

Truth be told, once someone begins Experiencing True Happiness, it's impossible to predict what will appear in Inner Space in response to what happens in Story Space.

If a child of yours were to die, it's likely that a "very intense" movement and frequency of energy would appear in Inner Space.

But it *can* appear ... it *can* be Experienced ... as the pure, raw experience it Truly is – without the "feel bad" story – and the overall emotional Experience *can* be very different.

I'm not saying you'd be "happy" or "glad," in the traditional sense, if a child died.

Of course not.

But I *am* saying that if you were Experiencing True Happiness at the time, you would simply be aware of a movement and frequency of energy in Inner Space – without names, labels, or "feel bad" judgments.

I say this as a parent of two children myself.

I say this after having many "challenging" experiences with my kids while Experiencing True Happiness that would ordinarily stimulate "bad feelings" in the lie, illusion, and story way of looking at things.

I also say this after experiencing the death of my father.

Until The Truth Virus completes a certain amount of its work, there's no way The Mind Machine (and therefore "you") will accept what I just shared at the idea and concept level – especially with such an "intense" experience as the death of a child.

The Mind Machine will just buzz and whirr and come back with lies, illusions, and stories like:

"That doesn't make sense."

Or …

"I don't agree."

Or …

"That couldn't be."

Or …

"That would be a cold and heartless response."

Or …

"I'd be a terrible person if I responded that way."

This is something that can and *must* be EXPERIENCED.

And it's not "cold and heartless" at all.

It's **The Truth.**

"Cold and heartless" and "terrible person" are just Mind Machine stories!

I expect this answer to be considered controversial by many who read it and allow it to swirl at the idea and concept level only.

Q: I have problems with my health that cause me a lot of discomfort and are the primary cause of my depression because they seem to be endless. What would you advise in this situation?

A: From my perspective, using the language and perspective I've shared here, this is what you're really saying:

There's a persistent illness accompanied by physical discomfort. The Mind Machine observes it and makes up a story about it being "endless" and the "negative" implications of that.

The movement of energy in Inner Space begins to move and vibrate at a specific frequency in response to the story about "endless" discomfort.

The Mind Machine observes that movement and frequency of emotional energy, buzzes and whirrs, and tells you a story that it's "depression" and it's "uncomfortable and bad."

Without the involvement of The Mind Machine, which is what happens when True Happiness is being Experienced, here's what would happen instead:

There's a persistent illness accompanied by physical discomfort.

The movement of energy in Inner Space begins to move and vibrate at a specific frequency in response to the illness and discomfort.

The movement and frequency of the emotional energy is simply Experienced, with no name, label, or judgment – not good, not bad, not pleasurable, not painful.

Just a movement and frequency of energy appearing in Inner Space.

I must also share that as difficult it may be for you to believe, it is also possible for The Truth Virus to have so much impact on The Mind Machine that you wouldn't even experience physical "pain" from the illness anymore.

I discuss this possibility in the final Chapter of the book called, "The Red Pill."

Like my answer to the question above about the death of a child, it's likely The Mind Machine will observe this answer, buzz, whirr, and kick out thoughts like, "There's no way I could ever be Okay with endless pain." or "Bullshit. I really am depressed about this." or "No, it really, really hurts. It's excruciating!"

If thoughts like that do appear, I get it.

I hear you.

I've been there in my own way.

All I can say is that when you actually EXPERIENCE True Happiness, you'll see that I'm telling The Truth.

As I stated, this is literally "mind blowing" stuff!

Q: I would be interested to know what your point of view is on people who say they're not aware of their emotions or don't feel them.

A: While working with thousands of people worldwide, I hear this from time to time. When I poke at it, when I explore it, what I see is that it's generally not true.

There can be exceptions, of course. I'm just talking about what I've seen.

From my experience, most people who *say* they don't experience emotions really do experience emotions. Lots of them. They may *appear* to be muffled or hidden from view, but they're there.

There's just a Mind Machine story running that says they're not being felt.

Why would The Mind Machine tell a story like that?

Because for some people, emotions are perceived as uncomfortable and scary.

As you now know, emotions aren't really uncomfortable or scary (except in a story), but it's a very compelling story for many people.

From my experience, energy moves in specific ways and is tuned to specific frequencies in *all of us* whether The Mind Machine kicks out a story saying it isn't happening or it's barely noticeable.

Q: For about 90 percent of my life, I'm emotionally neutral, and when emotional peaks appear, what I do is look for the meaning I'm assigning to the event, then see that I'm creating the meaning in my mind, and that dissolves the emotion. As a purely mental exercise, I find this beneficial for personal growth. How do you feel about that?

A: When it comes to Experiencing True Happiness, we're not talking about "dissolving" emotions or doing anything to them. That's the old game, the old path, and it ultimately leads nowhere.

When it comes to Experiencing True Happiness, we're talking about experiencing emotions, all of them, without names, labels, or judgmental stories.

To me, that's True personal growth.

I'm not saying there's no value to purely mental exercises.

I'm not saying, "Don't do them." They can be very helpful and supportive at certain stages of your journey.

All I'm saying is that purely mental exercises designed to manage, minimize, muffle, reframe, ignore, release, dissolve, destroy, transmute, heal core causes, or eliminate negative emotions will <u>not</u> lead to the Experience of True Happiness.

Purely mental exercises like that will keep you on the hamster wheel and forever chasing rabbits you'll never catch.

Q: Is the experience of True Happiness you describe, in essence, learning to detach from emotions and observe the ego?"

A: No. That's not what I'm saying.

It's true that I've invited you to observe what's appearing in Inner Space, and someone could say that what I'm calling The Mind Machine is the same thing as what others call ego.

But there's a BIG difference between observing what's appearing in Inner Space and the operation of The Mind Machine ... in the way I'm describing it ... and "detaching" from it.

Detachment, in its simplest form, means to be separate or disconnect from, which, in this context, would be another attempt to manage, minimize, muffle, reframe, ignore, release, dissolve, destroy, transmute, heal core causes, or eliminate negative emotions.

True Happiness is the extreme opposite of "detachment."

When experiencing True Happiness, you're *fully* immersed

in and connected to the movements and frequencies of energy in Inner Space.

But ...

The full immersion and connection is to the pure, raw experience, not the story.

Q: Does meditation help to achieve the state of True Happiness?

A: Many people will disagree with me on this, but my answer is "Not usually."

From what I've seen, Experienced myself, and been told by others who are brutally honest about their experiences, meditation is not a path that leads to True Happiness as it's defined here.

I'm speaking very generally, but what usually happens with meditation is that while someone is in a meditative state, The Mind Machine disengages, doesn't buzz and whirr, and Inner Space appears devoid of the movement of emotional energy ... or ... there's an appearance The Mind Machine labels as "peaceful" or "serene" and "good."

As soon as someone exits the meditative state and returns to waking consciousness, however, The Mind Machine re-engages and they experience the illusion of positive and negative emotions again.

Rarely does the cumulative effect of meditating for long period of time do anything to change how The Mind Machine operates.

There can always be exceptions, of course.

Q: What's the hardest part about changing your beliefs so you can experience True Happiness?

A: I realize that the idea, concept, and technique of changing beliefs is common in self-help and psychological models. However, that's not what I'm talking about here.

Let me explain.

To do that, let me share another metaphor – the metaphor of the sun and clouds.

Imagine that the sun represents True Happiness.

Imagine that the lies, illusions, and stories in The Mind Machine represent a solid, dense layer of cloud cover that blocks you from Experiencing the sun of True Happiness.

"Changing beliefs" would mean changing the content of the cloud cover. If you change what's in the cloud cover, no matter how "positive" or "empowering" it may be, there's still cloud cover in place that blocks the experience of the sun.

I'm talking about knocking out the cloud cover completely, so the sun of True Happiness can shine in.

It may seem like a subtle difference, but it's actually a HUGE difference.

Q: How do I know I'm on the right track if I don't use feelings or emotional reactions as "radar" anymore?

A: You're actually talking about two different things here.

When I speak of True Happiness, I'm speaking about Experiencing pure emotional energy without a Mind Machine story bonded to it.

When you say you use feelings as radar, you're talking about an appearance in Inner Space that has information attached to it, what you might call an "intuitive message" or a "hunch" or "inner guidance."

That message or guidance may appear to have a feeling attached to it, but it's the message and guidance that matters most.

That's a different experience than True Happiness.

An intuitive message or hunch or inner guidance, whether a feeling appears attached to it or not, isn't a story kicked out by the buzz-whirr of The Mind Machine as I've defined it.

It's something different, and it doesn't stop when True Happiness is being Experienced.

Intuitive messages will still come through, possibly attached to movements and frequencies of energy in Inner Space, possibly on their own.

Nothing is "lost" along these lines when you start Experiencing True Happiness.

Q: Our small prayer group has been spending a lot of time addressing and eliminating blocks and repeating patterns. How does True Happiness address blocks and patterns like that?

A: In a sense, The Truth Virus, as we've discussed it here, "eliminates" blocks and patterns as part of its function. The question here is, what sorts of "blocks" and "patterns" are you speaking of?

What your prayer group has been doing may be different, but in general, when people talk about eliminating blocks and lifetime patterns, they're talking about patterns like self-sabotage, struggling with money, repeating painful relationship dynamics, ups and downs in career, etc.

In general, working to eliminate blocks and patterns like that does NOT lead to the Experience of True Happiness.

To Experience True Happiness, The Mind Machine must be disengaged from hijacking and telling stories about pure, raw emotional experience.

That's generally very different from working to eliminate specific patterns and blocks.

Q: Can you say more about how Experiencing True Happiness can also affect my relationships, my money, my body, my health, etc.?

A: I could probably talk for 2 weeks about this, but I must be brief and general here.

All day, every day, you're focused on trying to change, fix, improve, create, or experience specific things in your life.

Happiness is the ultimate motivation behind all those attempts to change, fix, improve, create, or experience those specific things.

Therefore, every time you try to change, fix, improve, create, or experience something in your life, you're really trying to be happy. You think, "If I can just 'X', I'll be happy." So you work hard to achieve X.

Well, if you're already happy, Truly Happy, all the time, no matter what happens, what do you think happens to your list of things you want to change, fix, improve, create, or experience?

It'll change, right?

It'll shrink, right?

You may not believe it right now (meaning The Mind Machine buzzes and whirrs and kicks thoughts like these into Inner Space, "I'm not sure about that." or "I disagree with that."), but you'll see for yourself once you begin Experiencing True Happiness.

That's what happens.

The list shrinks.

Many wants and desires that were on the list simply drop off, and the ones that remain on the list are perceived very differently.

When you're Truly Happy all the time, the list shrinks, and the way you perceive the things that remain on your list (and whether you get them or not) changes.

It forms BIG drops in your pond that ripple out into every aspect of your life, including relationships, money, business and career, even body and health.

The impact of those ripples isn't something you can understand, figure out, get a sneak preview of, or project into in advance.

It's beyond words, ideas, and concepts.

It must be Experienced.

I need to make sure we're clear on something else at this point.

When the True Happiness drops start rippling out in your pond, it doesn't mean that you're going to suddenly become a millionaire, find your soul mate, or instantly fix a relationship that's been broken for years.

It doesn't mean a persistent health or body "problem" is

suddenly going to heal overnight.

It doesn't mean that whatever fantasy you have of what you'd love to see appear or disappear in your life is going to suddenly appear or disappear in your life.

Some or all of the examples I just shared *could* happen, but that's not what I mean about True Happiness waves rippling out through every aspect of your life.

There's no specific kind of transformation, detail, or change in Story Space that's guaranteed when True Happiness appears in Inner Space. The details can be all over the map, depending on the unique story you're starring in.

There's no one way it looks.

There's actually an infinite number of possibilities.

I feel it's best for you to be surprised and delighted (so to speak) when you actually Experience the True Happiness ripples yourself.

It's an extraordinary and, as I've said, literally mind-blowing Experience!

Q: What about love?

A: Wow. I could write an entire book on this topic alone. I'm going to answer this question fully, but I must warn you to be prepared for a "controversial" answer that many Mind Machines won't appear to "like."

The word "love" is used in so many different contexts and means many different things in the different contexts. For purposes of discussion here, there are three primary contexts and meanings for the word "love:"

1. A word used to describe your opinion about or preference for something *without* a movement or frequency of energy appearing in Inner Space (for example, "I love carrot cake.").

2. A word used to describe a movement or frequency of energy that appears in Inner Space related to another person or living being (for example, "I love my mother." or "I love my dog.").

3. A word used to describe "spiritual" dynamics (for example, "God is love.").

For our purposes here, I'm only going to discuss option number two, when love is used to describe a movement or frequency of energy that appears in Inner Space related to another person or living being.

At this point on our journey together, it may or may not surprise you to hear that when we use the word "love" with reference to a person or living being, it's really no different than using any other word to describe any other movement or frequency of energy appearing in Inner Space.

"Love" is used to describe a unique set of movements and frequencies in Inner Space that tend to be very strong and intense.

I say "set of movements" because what we call love isn't "one thing" – it can actually take various shapes and forms and still be called love.

In this sense, there's nothing Truly special about "love" in this context, except in a Mind Machine story.

Like all other emotional movements and frequencies, The Mind Machine simply observed specific movements and frequencies in Inner Space, learned to name them "love," and bonded a highly positive story to them.

If those specific movements and frequencies appear in Inner Space and you become aware of them, you say, "I love you."

If they don't appear, you don't use the word.

It's that simple, Truth be told.

In some cases, which happens a lot in romantic relationships, when those movements and frequencies once appeared but don't any longer, we say "I don't love you *any more*."

Don't take my word for this.

Look for yourself and See what's happening in Inner Space when you find yourself saying or feeling that you "love" someone.

KEY POINT:

This is in no way meant to minimize or demean love or loving. It's just an observation of The Truth of what you See if you examine that specific appearance with brutal honesty

KEY POINT:

Love doesn't go away when True Happiness waves begin to ripple out.

But what you call "love" can change and expand when True Happiness waves begin to ripple out – and a lot of what you would have once called "pain and confusion" related to love or loving (including when it isn't reciprocated by someone else) will drop away.

When True Happiness waves begin to ripple out, you will most likely continue to tell people and pets you love them when the "love movements and frequencies" appear.

I do.

All the time.

But the opportunity presented by True Happiness is:

▷ For you to be crystal clear on what you're *really* saying and what's *really* happening when you say or think, "I love ...."

▷ For the "love frequency" to appear more often than it does now.

▷ For the "love frequency" to no longer be *limited* to appearing only with specific people or living beings at specific times.

▷ For the "love frequency" to no longer appear and disappear with the same person or living being as appearances in Story Space change, and as The Mind Machine's stories about those appearances change over time.

Q: What about emotions in dreams? Is The Mind Machine still active there?

A: "Dream Space," as I call it, is a very unique "place." There are no rules or formulas about what happens there or what *can* happen there.

The best way to look at it is simply this:

Any time you experience emotions in Dream Space that have positive-negative, pleasurable-painful stories bonded to them, The Mind Machine is involved.

Q: What about deep sleep when everything seems to go black?

A: When you experience what's called deep sleep, which means total blackout, nothing is appearing in Inner Space or Story Space at all, so there's no movement or frequency of energy in Inner Space and The Mind Machine isn't active.

Q: You create a very compelling case for positive and negative emotions not being real. However, when I look into Inner Space, it still seems like some emotions feel good and others feel bad. What do you suggest?

A: When you look into Inner Space, it will continue to appear as if there are positive and negative emotions until The Truth Virus has been introduced and completed a certain amount of work.

That's just the way it is because The Mind Machine stories are so entrenched and mesmerizing.

However, once The Truth Virus has been introduced and progressed to a certain point, your "perceptions" will begin to change, then change more, then transform into an Experience of True Happiness.

Q: How long do I need to watch and wait for the pure, raw experience and the story to separate and to Experience True Happiness?

A: There's no way to predict this. If we were to track the lives of 1,000 people who embraced what's being shared here, and monitored how long it took to move through The Truth Virus stages I'll be describing, we'd see all sorts of manifestations.

You are here as a unique individual Experiencing the unfolding of a unique story you call "my life."

The only thing I can promise is that if Experiencing True Happiness is part of your story, it will happen at the "best" time for you and in the "best" way.

Q: How do I know if The Truth Virus is working?

A: You may not know it's working in the early stages. You may even think, "nothing is happening."

But if The Truth Virus has been introduced and is allowed to do its work, the day will come when you'll know it's "working" beyond the shadow of any doubt.

Why?

Because your perception and Experience of what's happening in Inner Space will change radically.

That concludes this batch of questions and answers.

Once The Truth Virus has been introduced into The Mind Machine and had some time to make changes, you'll begin to see things change in Inner Space, but you'll perceive it as a "work in progress" for a while.

There's a gap separating where you are now from actually experiencing True Happiness on a consistent basis.

That gap must be bridged, and the bridge is built in several stages.

To discover what the stages are and what to expect as you move through them, turn the page.

CHAPTER
8

Bridging The Gap

When you first opened this book, you were at what I call "Point A," which means The Mind Machine was in a fully operational state, running on autopilot, using its magic trick to create the illusion of positive and negative emotions and a war against the "feel bad" emotions.

If you're resonating with what I've shared here, then you want to get to "Point B," which means that The Truth Virus has done its work and you're experiencing **True Happiness** consistently.

The gap between Point A and Point B is a HUGE one.

The Mind Machine has been running on autopilot for as long as you've been alive.

While it's always learning and updating its database, programs, and algorithms, it tends to become extremely rigid as it relates to emotions once you reach a certain age.

There's so much stored in The Mind Machine database that supports the illusion of positive and negative emotions, and the illusion of feel-good and feel-bad emotions, and there's a lot of momentum keeping The Mind Machine operating the "old way."

As I stated, you could compare that dynamic to how much force and energy a rocket must expend to overcome the resistance of gravity and free itself to fly in space.

All journeys into True Happiness are unique, but there tends to be several common stages that people experience as a bridge is built from Point A to Point B – as lies, illusions, and stories are converted into a direct Experience of Truth.

The stages are:

1. Introduction Of The Truth Virus

2. Destabilization Of The Mind Machine

3. Adaptation

4. Stabilization Of The Mind Machine

5. True Happiness

Let's look at each of the stages individually.

Introduction Of The Truth Virus

We discussed this stage in a previous chapter. The only question is …

> Will what's shared here be accepted and will The
> Truth Virus be allowed to begin its work?

Destabilization Of The Mind Machine

As The Truth Virus works its way through The Mind Machine, many things can appear. You could think of The Mind Machine as being "unstable" during this stage.

In case the virus metaphor doesn't work as well for you, let me share two more metaphors to illustrate what I mean by "unstable."

First, I'll share the metaphor of a ceiling fan.

Imagine you have a ceiling fan in your bedroom. Imagine it's running and the blades are rotating at high speed.

What would happen if you took a stick and shoved it into the fan blades?

You'd hear a loud noise, the blade movement would slow down temporarily, and the normal operation of the fan "machine" would be interrupted by the stick.

However, the motor would still be running, so the fan blades would "try" to keep moving despite the disruption.

If the blades were moving fast enough when you shoved the stick into them, some of them might break, but the motor would keep buzzing and whirring and rotating the remaining blades.

If you shoved enough sticks into the fan blade and motor, and disrupted the operation of the fan enough, it would stop running altogether.

The Mind Machine is like the fan and The Truth Virus is like the sticks.

Second, I'll share the metaphor of an assembly line in an automobile factory.

With an assembly line, a mechanical platform moves to carry the parts of an automobile that need to be assembled by people or robotic machines.

What would happen if you threw a wrench into the mechanism that propels the mechanical platform?

The assembly line wouldn't stop right away, but you'd hear a lot of noise, the assembly line movement would sputter, some of the automobile pieces would fall off the platform, and the smooth operation of the assembly line would be disrupted.

Continue to throw wrenches into that mechanism, it would stop running altogether, and none of the automobiles would be assembled correctly.

Think of The Mind Machine as the mechanism propelling the mechanical platform and The Truth Virus as the wrenches.

The key here is that neither the fan nor the assembly line will stop working immediately. The sticks and wrenches will disrupt the normal operation, and if the disruption continues, over time, it will then stop operations completely.

The Truth Virus works in a similar way.

Adaptation

After The Truth Virus has done *some* of its work, when The Mind Machine asks its three questions, the answers either won't come lightning fast, they'll be different, or they'll be more complicated.

When The Mind Machine operated the "old way" on autopilot, it would observe an appearance of energy movement and frequency in Inner Space, buzz-whirr, and say, 'This is anger, and this doesn't feel good."

After The Truth Virus has had some impact, the output will change.

I want to give you several examples of the likely changes, but note that I'm taking creative liberties with the "mental dialog" to illustrate important points.

After The Truth Virus has completed *some* of its work, you might see thoughts like these appear in Inner Space:

"This is depression and it feels bad ... No, wait a minute, maybe that's not true. Maybe it's just a movement of energy and it feels fine..."

Or ...

"This is a movement of energy vibrating at a specific frequency. No, I'm not sure about that. It still feels like depression."

Or ...

"You really pissed me off when you said ____. Wait a minute. Am I *really* pissed off?"

Or ...

"I'm feeling really blue today. Blue? Is that *really* what I'm feeling? What's the pure, raw experience without the story?"

Or, the final example ...

"What *is* this? I'm not even sure anymore"

You get the idea.

There are many possible variations on the types of thoughts I just shared. They're for illustration purposes only. I'm sure your own unique thoughts will appear in Inner Space as The Truth Virus works its way through The Mind Machine.

This might seem silly or unbelievable to you, but a dialog like I just shared really does appear in Inner Space when The Mind Machine is in the adaptation stage.

I saw it on my own journey and heard about it when others narrated the details of their journeys to me.

Knowing what you now know, it's kind of funny to watch, Truth be told.

Why does this happen? Three reasons:

1. There's new data in The Mind Machine's database.

2. The Mind Machine programs and algorithms have been changed dramatically.

3. Just like the stick shoved into the fan and the wrench in the assembly line's drive mechanism, the normal operation of The Mind Machine has been disrupted, and it's struggling to come up with new rules and formulas to operate by so it can return to operating on autopilot again.

If you think of The Mind Machine for a moment as if it was a person, you might say that when it was running the "old way," it was confident and now it's not.

Now it's "insecure" about the answers to the three questions.

KEY POINT:

The Mind Machine observes EVERYTHING that appears in Inner Space, including itself.

When The Mind Machine observes itself buzzing and whirring and popping out conflicting outputs during this stage, "This is anger." then "Maybe this isn't anger." or "This is a movement of energy." then "No, this really is depression"– it recycles the three questions about its own conflicting outputs, and that …

Turbocharges The Truth Virus once again

Knowing what you now know, this too can be quite humorous to watch.

As The Mind Machine buzzes, whirrs, destabilizes, and recycles its own destabilization during this stage, it can actually appear to feel disorienting, surreal, or uncomfortable to *YOU*.

If that appears, and it may not, you have the opportunity to observe it, do your best to See The Truth of what's going on, and ride the waves of change knowing it's just a stage that will pass.

It may also appear as if The Mind Machine is fighting The Truth Virus, trying to retain the status quo or resisting The Truth Virus. If it appears that way, it's just an illusion.

It's not what's really happening.

To get a really good feeling for and insight into what's *really* happening during the Adaptation stage, as The Truth Virus works through The Mind Machine and The Mind Machine observes things changing, I strongly recommend watching a video clip from a movie called *War Games* with Matthew Broderick.

I posted a copy of that clip on my website. Please go to the following page and you'll get immediate access to the video:

http://www.robertscheinfeld.com/wargames/

If it's quick and convenient for you to do it, I strongly recommend you stop reading for a moment and go watch the *War Games* video clip right now. It will be very supportive if you do that *before* continuing.

Another thing that can appear during this phase is that you can feel like The Mind Machine is your enemy, is against you, or is intentionally trying to drive you crazy or keep you from Experiencing True Happiness.

That's not True.

I call it The Mind *Machine* because it operates like a machine. It's not a person. It has no wants, desires, goals, or intentions – malicious or kind.

It's not for you or against you.

It just does what it was designed to do.

To discover more about why The Mind Machine was designed to do what it does, be sure to check out Appendix A of this book called "The Big Why."

Stabilization

After passing through the Adaptation stage, The Mind Machine stabilizes.

If you watched the video clip from the *War Games* movie, this was illustrated when the computer, after buzzing, whirring, and "learning," said, "A strange game. The only winning move is not to play. How about a nice game of chess?"

When The Mind Machine operated the "old way," it observed pure, raw emotional experiences in Inner Space, buzzed and whirred, created stories about them, and bonded the stories to the pure, raw experiences.

In the Stabilization phase, The Truth Virus has made so many modifications to The Mind Machine, that what appears in Inner Space changes in HUGE ways.

While all journeys are unique, it's likely you'll witness something like this in the early segments of the Stabilization stage:

1. The Mind Machine will observe movements and frequencies of energy in Inner Space.

2. It will ask its three questions.

3. It will answer them based on new data, new programs, and revised algorithms.

4. It will pop The Truth about the pure, raw experiences

into Inner Space versus the old lies, illusions, and stories (that is, these are just movements and frequencies of energy and are all welcome, even pleasurable).

Early in the Stabilization stage, you may still observe Mind Machine noise and chattering, a mix of old and new thoughts about emotions, but it won't feel as chaotic, congested, confusing, complex, or "intense" as it did in the Adaptation stage.

In this stage, you may also notice that you're Experiencing True Happiness a lot or in blips, The Mind Machine observes it and still wants to label it. But if that happens, it tends to be quiet, just a hint or echo of what it used to be.

During the final segments of the Stabilization stage (although it *can* happen in the Adaptation or True Happiness stages), it's likely that additional waves of Experience will ripple out.

The ripples will take the shapes of additional questions asked by The Mind Machine. There are many variations of how this dynamic can appear, but in general, it will be something like this:

"I feel like a stranger in a strange world. I'm experiencing True Happiness, but everyone around me – friends, family, business associates – is perceiving and talking about emotions the old way. What do I do about this? What do I say to them? How do I respond when they ask me how I feel about things? How do I respond when they're surprised I'm not getting angry, hurt, embarrassed, etc.?"

Or ...

"Shouldn't I tell *everyone* about this? If I could save them from experiencing all the pain of negative emotions, especially my friends and family, I should."

For all questions and appearances like this, here's what to keep in mind:

▷ It's just the Mind Machine buzzing and whirring and trying to reorganize its files in response to the work of The Truth Virus.

▷ The feeling of being an alien, different, isolated, etc. is a blip that will pass as it dissolves into the Experience of True Happiness.

▷ In terms of sharing this with others, that's certainly a gift you *can* give others, and I encourage you to do it. But remember that you may or may not see this message being resisted or rejected. Why? Because it's not part of everyone's life story to experience True Happiness – now or at all.

▷ All of this will take care of itself as time passes and your story unfolds.

As The Truth Virus continues its work, your Experience will then move into the final stage…

True Happiness

In this stage, pure, raw emotional experiences simply appear in Inner Space, with no story at all from The Mind Machine – not even a "true" one.

You will perceive something like this:

▷ Movements and frequencies of energy appear in Inner Space.

▷ The Mind Machine observes them.

▷ It does <u>not</u> buzz or whirr.

▷ It does <u>not</u> ask or answer the three questions.

▷ It just allows pure, raw experiences to "be."

▷ You will be aware of the pure, raw experience only.

What this means, and you may find it hard to believe at this point, is that you just perceive ALL movements and frequencies of energy in Inner Space as just that – movements and frequencies of emotional energy in Inner Space.

No words or labels will appear.

While you'll remember that you once used them, and how impactful and "real" they once appeared, the old names – anger, fear, frustration, happiness, serenity, sadness, depression – permanently drop out of your Experience.

No positive-negative, good-bad judgments will appear in Inner Space.

You're Experiencing True Happiness .

All the time ...

No matter what's going on around you.

That'll be a BIG day for you!

It was for me and everyone else who has Experienced The Truth Virus in action.

It's now time to dot a few i's and cross a few t's, then I'll leave you for now, to Experience the full force of The Truth Virus.

When you're ready to dot those i's and cross those t's, *and then* find out what "The Red Pill" is all about, turn the page.

CHAPTER
9

Dotting I's and Crossing T's

The term "dotting i's and crossing t's" generally refers to taking care of the final details prior to the completion of a project or task.

We have some i's to dot and some t's to cross too.

Based on my experience, the following are possible options for how you'll respond at this point on our journey together:

▷ The content of this book is accepted *at the idea and concept level*, but will ultimately be ignored.

▷ The content is rejected at the idea and concept level.

▷ The Truth Virus partially deploys.

▷ The Truth Virus fully deploys.

However and whenever you respond, there's no right or wrong, good or bad option for you.

As I've shared multiple times, our stories and journeys are all unique, and True Happiness is not written into all of our stories – as odd as that might sound.

One of the options may be chosen immediately, or there may be a delay before the chosen one surfaces.

We'll take a look at the options individually in a minute, but first I want to build a foundation for what follows.

People who buy books like this one – that is, people who have a passion for personal or spiritual growth – tend to group into three types I call:

> ▷ Collectors
>
> ▷ Doers
>
> ▷ Transformers

Collectors

Collectors go from book to book, seminar to seminar, video to video, audio to audio, etc., collecting ideas and concepts.

Collectors really love collecting.

They really love what's perceived to be the fun of dancing with ideas and concepts for the sheer pleasure of dancing.

For Collectors, everything remains at the intellectual or theoretical level, and they seldom if ever experience lasting results or transformation.

They just collect.

Most Collectors have no idea that's all they're doing.

Doers

Doers go from technique to technique, strategy to strategy, taking action in an attempt to change, fix, and improve specific aspects of their lives.

Most Doers never find the techniques or strategies that actually end up creating permanent and True Transformation.

They just stay busy "doing."

Most doers would say they really want to get results, but The Truth is, they love "doing" more.

Transformers

After being a Collector or Doer for a while, or directly, some people become Transformers, which means they end up Experiencing and Knowing Truth.

If you want to know more about Collectors, Doers, and Transformers, head over to one of my blog posts here:

http://www.robertscheinfeld.com/types/

Having laid that foundation, let's now discuss the options for what may appear for you as you reach the conclusion of this book.

The Content Of This Book Is Accepted At The Idea And Concept Level, But Will Ultimately Be Ignored.

If you're a Collector, and you remain a Collector after reading this book, then the first possibility is that The Mind Machine will buzz and whirr, accept what I've shared here at the idea and concept level only, perceive that it "learned" something important, and then say something like:

"That's interesting."

Or ...

"That's fascinating."

Or ...

"That's way cool."

But you'll end up putting the book down and continuing to collect other ideas and concepts, without The Truth Virus ever deploying.

If this happens, it's because – as I explained – it's not part of your story to actually Experience True Happiness right now (or ever), but it was part of your story to have what was shared here be included in The Mind Machine's database – for whatever reason.

The Content Is Rejected At The Idea And Concept Level.

This possibility is similar to the previous one, but here, The Mind Machine buzzes and whirrs, rejects what was shared here at the idea and concept level, and you'll end up putting the book down and continuing on your journey, without The Truth Virus ever deploying.

If that happens, it's because, as I explained, again, it's not part of your story to actually Experience True Happiness right now (or ever), but it was part of your story to have what was shared here be included in The Mind Machine's database – for whatever reason.

The Truth Virus Partially Deploys.

It's possible that what was shared here will be accepted, The Truth Virus will begin to deploy, but then stop before it completes its work.

Why would that happen?

There are many possibilities, but here's the most typical scenario of what you'd observe appearing in Inner Space:

▷ Deployment begins with the Mind Machine still appearing to be "skeptical" about the Truthfulness of what was shared here.

▷ As The Truth Virus begins to deploy, The Mind Machine looks for "proof" to overcome its skepticism.

▷ Before The Truth Virus has enough time to do enough work, The Mind Machine will appear to decide it didn't find enough proof, and The Truth Virus will stop running.

Please understand, The Mind Machine has no power here. It can't stop The Truth Virus by itself. I described this possibility in this way because that's how it can appear to you in Inner Space.

If this happens, it's because, as I explained, it's not part of your story to actually Experience True Happiness right now (or ever), but it was part of your story to have The Truth Virus modify some of the Mind Machine's data, programs, and algorithms – for whatever reason – before it stops running.

The Truth Virus Fully Deploys.

This, of course, is the final possibility, and what this book was designed, ultimately, to do.

If this happens, it's because it *IS* part of your story to actually Experience True Happiness right now, and you'll go through the various stages I narrated in previous chapters until you Experience True Happiness.

I now want to repeat something I asserted several times in this book.

I've experienced EVERYTHING I've narrated in this book.

All the appearances.

All the stages.

Everything.

My style of teaching has always been:

1. Been there.
2. Done that.
3. Experience it to a very deep degree personally.
4. Pop up and offer a "debrief" of what I Saw and Experienced to others.

The details of the journey into the Experience of True Happiness came from me observing what actually happened to me and from what I later observed happening to others with whom I shared it.

It's not ideas, concepts, or theory.

This journey has been one of the most extraordinary Experiences I've ever had. If you take the journey, it's very likely you'll say the same thing.

It's now time to dot a one final i and cross one final t.

There's a lot I shared here.

And there's a lot I left out.

Intentionally.

Why?

Four reasons:

1. This book was designed to offer an opportunity for The Truth Virus to be introduced into your Mind Machine, and that's it.

2. A certain amount of detail is required to make that possible, but beyond that, it's just "collecting" and isn't necessary ... at this point.

3. I wanted to make this book a quick, easy read for the conscious part of you that's aware of the words that are superimposed over The Truth Virus. Longer books with long, dense paragraphs can be intimidating to some readers.

4. Making the book a quick, easy read also tends to increase the odds that it'll be read multiple times which would be very supportive in this case.

Okay. It's now time to find out what the heck "The Red Pill" I've been talking about is and why it might … or might not … be supportive for you to take it.

To find out, turn the page.

CHAPTER
10

The Red Pill

My goal in writing this book was to support you in Experiencing True Happiness, all the time, no matter what's going on around you.

And ...

To open a gateway to allow you to go beyond that, if you want to.

No matter what it takes.

For some people, this book alone can do that.

For some people, this book alone can introduce The Truth Virus into The Mind Machine and fully deploy it – leading to the Experience of True Happiness.

I expected – and intended – that to be the case for the majority of readers.

In sharing this message with thousands of people throughout the world, however, I've seen that for some people, the data, programs, and algorithms in The Mind Machine are so strong, so hypnotic, so mesmerizing, that it takes something more to introduce or fully deploy The Truth Virus.

To work "the magic."

This book didn't exist when it was time for The Truth Virus to be introduced and fully deployed within my own Mind Machine.

In my case, I had to travel a path that offered me the "something more" I just described.

In my case, I had to travel a path where I was given "The Red Pill."

Since that's what it took for me to Experience True Happiness on a consistent basis (and to go beyond it to Experience and "BE" in Truth in many other ways), it *might* be supportive for you too.

That's why I added this chapter.

What's The Red Pill?

Let me explain it this way.

In the film, *The Matrix*, the two main characters, Morpheus and Neo, have a conversation that's pivotal to the story.

If you've never seen the first movie in *The Matrix* trilogy, I strongly encourage you to go out and buy or rent a copy and watch it immediately after finishing this book (or watch it again if it's been a while since you've seen it).

You'll find it to be EXTREMELY supportive to our purposes here.

Here's what Morpheus said to Neo in that conversation:

You take the blue pill, the story ends, you wake up in your bed and believe whatever you want to believe. You take The

Red Pill, you stay in Wonderland, and I show you how deep the rabbit hole goes.

Neo chose The Red Pill.

After swallowing The Red Pill, Neo didn't have to do anything himself at first. The Red Pill did all the work by triggering a series of events that freed him from the lie, illusion, and story called "The Matrix."

After being freed, he was ultimately able to Experience The Truth, his destiny of being "The One," and for new sources of creative power to be expressed through him that re-shaped his life and world.

After The Red Pill worked its magic and Neo "woke up" to The Truth, he had to take action to adjust to The Truth, to discover and develop what he was Truly capable of as "The One."

The same can true for you … *if* it's needed … and *if* it would be supportive.

Beyond what you'll receive from this book (which I expect to be a lot), I can give you a Red Pill that will support the deployment of The Truth Virus … and … help you with adjusting, discovering, and developing what you're Truly capable of, and enabling new sources of creative power to surge through you and re-shape your life and world – just like Neo in The Matrix.

The Red Pill offers three significant benefits:

1. If this book did <u>not</u> introduce The Truth Virus and allow it to fully deploy, The Red Pill can complete the job or get it done.

2. If this book *did* introduce The Truth Virus, The Red Pill can dramatically accelerate how it moves through The Mind Machine

3. If this book *did* introduce The Truth Virus and allow it to fully deploy, The Red Pill can help you go deeper into an Experience of what "Being In Truth" really means.

Why?

Because The Mind Machine doesn't just engage, buzz-whirr, and hijack emotions.

It engages, buzzes and whirrs, hijacks, and kicks out lies, illusions and stories about every other aspect of your experience too.

Continuing the metaphor, you could say there's another strain of The Truth Virus that can be introduced into The Mind Machine that re-writes files, deletes files, re-writes programs and algorithms, and installs new programs and algorithms that dramatically affect what happens to you, and how you perceive everything else that happens to you.

In short, what I call "Being In Truth" goes way beyond just being Truly Happy all the time (which is HUGE on its own).

It also affects every other aspect of your life, Inner Space, and Story Space.

KEY POINT:

> The Red Pill can introduce and fully deploy the additional strain of The Truth Virus.

Let me explain what The Red Pill is like by sharing two more metaphors.

The first metaphor is that of peeling a hard-boiled egg.

I like hard-boiled eggs.

But when I was younger, I could never seem to peel off the shell without mangling the egg inside.

Then someone showed me how to do it.

First you take the egg and crack it all over the shell by gently tapping it against a hard surface.

Then you put the palm of your hand over the cracked shell and gently roll it back and forth. That helps separate the thin membrane that connects the shell to the egg.

Then, if you cracked it just right, and rolled it just right, the shell easily pulls away from the egg (the "prize" inside), and you can eat the entire egg.

Using this metaphor, imagine that:

1. The eggshell represents The Mind Machine operating the old way, creating the illusion of positive-feel-good-emotions and negative-feel-bad-emotions.
2. The crack-crack-crack-roll-roll-roll is The Red Pill.
3. The egg inside is the "prize," True Happiness and Being In Truth.

By cracking the eggshell just right (coming at it from multiple angles), rolling it just right, and sliding off the eggshell just right, True Happiness and Being In Truth are revealed and become a consistent Experience.

The second metaphor is that of demolishing a building using explosive charges.

It takes months, sometimes years to build large buildings from the ground up. But if a specific kind of explosive charge is placed in specific locations within the building and detonated in a specific way, the building can be demolished – brought straight down – in a matter of seconds.

I posted a video for you on my website to show this in action so you can get a good visual and feeling for what I'm talking about:

http://www.robertscheinfeld.com/demolition/

I strongly suggest that you stop reading for a moment and watch that video clip before continuing.

Using this metaphor, imagine that:

1. The building represents The Mind Machine operating the old way, creating the illusion of positive-feel-good-emotions and negative-feel-bad-emotions.

2. The explosive charges represent The Red Pill.

3. When the building is brought down, it opens a gateway into the Experience of True Happiness and Being In Truth.

So, what the heck is The Red Pill?

It's an Experience I created.

A 24-week Experience that, like Neo taking The Red Pill, sets many things into motion that cause multiple strains of The Truth Virus to fully deploy, complete their work, and take you into Experiencing True Happiness, and then beyond it into Being In Truth with everything in your life.

A 24-week Experience that provides the crack-crack-crack-roll-roll-roll to the eggshell for you.

A 24-week Experience that provides the explosive charges, then places and detonates them in just the right way.

A 24-week Experience with coaching components built in so you can interact with me personally as part of introducing and fully deploying multiple strains of The Truth Virus.

I created a special video for you here if you want to know more about The Red Pill:

http://www.robertscheinfeld.com/the-red-pill/

Our journey here together is almost done.

To hear about how to hit the ground running, turn the page.

CHAPTER
11

Hitting The Ground Running

Wow.

We've come a long way together, baby!

Here are a few final thoughts to support you in hitting the ground running when you set this book down.

Remember

The vast majority of what appeared in Inner Space while you read this book, and what appears *after* you put it down will <u>only</u> be:

▷ The buzz-whirr of The Mind Machine …

▷ "Old" thoughts, stories and conclusions …

▷ Based on "old" data, programs, and algorithms in The Mind Machine …

▷ The Big Opportunity for you now is to:

▷ Actually look into Inner Space, see what's really *going* on, then See what's really going on.

▷ Actually look into Inner Space and allow pure, raw experience to separate from The Mind Machine's stories about it …

▷ Versus thinking about it, analyzing it, trying to understand it or figure it out, focusing only on ideas, concepts, and theories.

Be Patient

Easier said than done, I know.

Believe me, I know.

But it's also important.

There's no single way to take the journey into **True Happiness**.

Assuming it's going to happen, there's no way to predict when The Truth Virus will begin its work, when its work will become visible to you, or when the work will be completed.

It may be really quick or it may not.

If you find yourself being impatient, what's REALLY happening?

Just Mind Machine buzz-whirr-noise!

It'll ultimately quiet down and dissolve.

Trust

I stated that you are a unique character who is the star of a unique, extraordinary story.

I didn't talk about this in earlier Chapters because it's off the topic for this book, but I want to plant the seed now that there's an "Intelligence," a "Consciousness," a "Force" – whatever you want to call it – that's driving what happens to you in your story, just like fiction writers drive what happens in their stories.

That "Author" wrote into your story that your character would read this book to this point.

That Author had a reason for that and a plan for you.

You can trust that whatever impact this book was meant to have, it will have, *when it's meant to.*

If you find yourself unable to trust in that, if you find yourself doubting, worried, or desiring to control, manage, or speed up The Truth Virus surfacing, what is it?

Just Mind Machine buzz-whirr-noise!

To learn more about who the Author is, the role it plays, and how it relates to you, I suggest taking The Red Pill.

Be Sure To Experience <u>All</u> The Bonus Content

Throughout the book, and summarized in Appendix E, I shared a variety of links to pages on my websites that contain bonus material to support your journey into the True Happiness Experience.

Be sure to Experience all the bonus materials as soon as possible, if you haven't already.

I promise you it will be well worth your while!

Reminder Of Key Points

Finally, I want to remind you one more time of these six key points:

1. Everything I've shared here is **Real and True.**

2. I've actually experienced <u>everything</u> I shared here.

3. I'm Experiencing True Happiness, all day, every day,

right here, right now.

4. Other people have gotten "there" too by embracing what's shared here.

5. No hype, fluff, bullshit, or sizzle without the steak.

6. You can get "there" too – no matter what noise The Mind Machine may kick into Inner Space.

So now, BIG drops have been dropped into your pond and the most supportive ripples for your unique journey are rippling out.

I've done all I can do through this book.

From this moment on, it's up to you and the Author of your story.

From this moment on, what happens, happens.

Cool …

Enjoy the journey!

Oh yeah, when this book has Experiential impact on you, I'd love to hear your story. Just visit this page on my website and send me a message:

http://www.robertscheinfeld.com/contact/

I'd like to close by expressing my appreciation to you for spending so much of your valuable time with me here.

I trust you've found it to be time "well spent."

On that note, I'll say "Bye-Bye" for now and will look forward to our next form of contact, whatever shape that may take.

APPENDIX

A

The Big Why

At various points in the book, I asserted:

▷ There's a reason The Mind Machine was created to operate as it does.

▷ There's a reason the operation of The Mind Machine can be modified to allow True Happiness to be Experienced.

▷ There's an Author who has been "writing" your story all along and will continue to write it, with specific objectives in mind.

If you want to know about "The Big Why" behind those statements, I created a special document for you to read.

You can download it here:

http://www.robertscheinfeld.com/the-big-why/

APPENDIX

B

Glossary Of Terms

(In Alphabetical Order)

Algorithm

A process or set of rules to be followed in calculations or other problem-solving operations, especially by a computer.

Appearance

The label used to describe anything that appears in Inner Space or Story Space – person, place, thing, thought, emotion, sensation, etc.

Deep Sleep

The label used to describe a state of consciousness where nothing appears in Inner Space or Story Space and The Mind Machine doesn't engage.

Dream Space

The label used to describe the "space" in which dreams appear to take place. Dream Space is a subset of Inner Space.

Emotions

The label used to describe the movement and frequency of energy in Inner Space.

Experience

Experience with a capital "E" or underlined "E" refers to an Experience of Truth, an Experience of "What's Really Happening," versus lies, illusions, and stories created by The Mind Machine about What's Really Happening.

Feelings

A synonym for emotion.

Frequency Of Energy

A label used to describe part of what makes each emotion appear unique.

Happiness

One specific frequency that the movement of energy in Inner Space gets tuned to.

Human Story or Human Game

The label used to describe all aspects of what is commonly called The Human Experience.

Inner Space

A label used to describe the vast space that appears to be inside of us, separate from Story Space, in which thoughts, emotions, and sensations appear.

Judgment

A label used to describe thoughts kicked into Inner Space

by The Mind Machine that tell a story of duality and polarity – good and bad, right and wrong, better and worse, positive and negative, etc.

Judgmental Stories

The stories The Mind Machine tells about the pure, raw experiences it observes in Inner Space and Story Space.

Know

Knowing with a capital "K" is a label used to describe an Experience that involves perceiving or being aware of something from the perspective of Truth, from the perspective of What's Really Happening, versus the lies, illusions, and stories kicked out by The Mind Machine about What's Really Happening. Knowing goes way beyond what's commonly called "understanding."

Labels

Words that are used to describe appearances in Inner Space or Story Space. They are never what they point to. They simply point to something and attempt to describe it for practical purposes in conversation and communication. Examples: anger and frustration for emotions; chair, car, and mountain for objects; hair, eyes, and nose for a body, etc.

Lies, Illusions, and Stories

Another label used to describe the output of The Mind Machine, the stories it bonds to pure, raw experience.

Movement Of Energy

A Truthful definition of what an emotion really is.

Names

Words that are used to describe appearances in Inner Space or Story Space. They are never what they point to. They simply point to something and attempt to describe it for practical purposes in conversation and communication. Examples: anger and frustration for emotions; chair, car, and mountain for objects; hair, eyes, and nose for a body, etc.

see (with a lowercase "s")

The label used to describe what you see with your eyes, or what is seen through the distorted lens of lies, illusions, and stories.

See

A label used to describe perceiving fully from the perspective of Truth, from "What's Really Happening," versus the lies, illusions and stories about What's Happening kicked out by The Mind Machine. Seeing goes way beyond seeing with the eyes or understanding something.

Sensation

A label used to describe appearances in Inner Space related to the body.

Story Space

The place where people, places, things, and your own body appear to be. It's called "Story" Space because of the metaphor of your life being a story just like you see in written works of fiction, TV shows, movies, plays, and video games.

The Mind Machine

A label used to describe the mechanism through which

appearances in Inner Space and Story space are separated, described, named and judged.

The Red Pill

A 24-week experience that supports the deployment and acceleration of The Truth Virus and takes you into the True Happiness Experience and beyond.

Thought

An appearance in Inner Space that that tells a story in the shape of words, still photographs, videos, sounds, or voices.

True Happiness

A label used to describe experiencing the movements and frequencies of emotional energy without names, labels, descriptions, judgments, or cause-and-effect stories.

Truth

A label used to point to and describe What's Really Happening in Inner Space, Story Space, and behind the scenes that's The Source of everything we are and experience.

APPENDIX
C

Give Others A Great Gift

If you resonated with what you read here, and most importantly, if you're Seeing The Truth of what was shared, please give the gift of this book by spreading the word to other people you know and care about.

To do that, you can:

1. Send Them To The Official Website For The Book ...

To watch videos and get more information on the book:

http://www.happinessbook.com/

2. Send Them Directly To Amazon ...

http://www.happinessbook.com/amazon/

3. Send Them To Their Favorite Bookstore ...

To buy physical copies of the book.

4. Gift A Copy Of The Book To Others ...

To friends, family, loved ones, even business associates.

5. Spread The Word And Share Through Your Social Media Accounts ...

Link to the preceding websites on your Facebook, Twitter, and/or other social network pages.

What better gift can you give someone you care about than the gift of being **Truly Happy**, all the time, no matter what's going on?

If You Buy Multiple Copies Yourself

Please send an email with proof of purchase to the following email address and I'll reply with a special thank-you gift:

copies@happinessbook.com

I very much appreciate the efforts of people who help us spread this important "word"!

APPENDIX
D

Resources

Here are some additional resources within my sphere of influence that might interest you:

Main Website

http://www.robertscheinfeld.com/

Main Blog

http://www.robertscheinfeld.com/blog/

Main Email List

http://www.robertscheinfeld.com/email-list/

***The Ultimate Key To Happiness* Book Readers List**

http://www.happinessbook.com/subscribe/

This list will keep you up-to-date and also give you a link to a secret Facebook group page that provides additional tips, insights, support, connections with other readers, and more.

Facebook

http://www.robertscheinfeld.com/facebook/

Twitter

http://www.robertscheinfeld.com/twitter/

The Red Pill

http://www.robertscheinfeld.com/the-red-pill/

Private And Group Coaching

http://www.happinessbook.com/coaching/

***The Ultimate Key To Happiness* Multimedia Experience**

http://www.robertscheinfeld.com/happy-experience/

***The Ultimate Key To Happiness* Audiobook**

http://www.robertscheinfeld.com/audio-books/

Introduction To My Other Teachings

http://www.robertscheinfeld.com/teachings/

iPhone, iPad, and Android Apps To Support You

http://www.robertscheinfeld.com/apps

APPENDIX

E

Summary Of Bonus Links

In the preceding pages of the book, I noted several websites where you can access bonus materials designed to augment your Experience of this book.

Here's a summary of those links and what they'll give you:

Video Examples Of The Mind Machine In Action

http://www.happinessbook.com/video-examples/

Robert's Email List For Readers Of The Book

http://www.happinessbook.com/subscribe/

***War Games* Video Clip**

http://www.robertscheinfeld.com/wargames/

Collectors, Doers, and Transformers Blog Post

http://www.robertscheinfeld.com/types/

Video Of A Building Being Demolished By Explosive Charges

http://www.robertscheinfeld.com/demolition/

A Detailed Explanation Of The Red Pill

http://www.robertscheinfeld.com/the-red-pill/

Share Your Story With Robert

http://www.robertscheinfeld.com/contact/

Download "The Big Why" Document

http://www.robertscheinfeld.com/the-big-why/

Like To Have A Multimedia Experience Of The Book?

Go Deeper, And Turbocharge The Truth Virus ...
http://www.robertscheinfeld.com/happy-experience/

CPSIA information can be obtained at www.ICGtesting.com
Printed in the USA
BVOW08s0223020716

453906BV00002B/76/P